City Limits

City Limits

Walking Portland's Boundary

David Oates

with contributions from
William Ashworth
David Bragdon
David Hassin
Holly Iburg and Gary Conkling
Eric Lemelson
Kathleen Dean Moore
Kelly Rodgers
Ana Maria Spagna

Parts of the chapter "Epilogue: A Democracy of Water" appeared in *Earth Island Journal*, Spring 2005.

The paper in this book meets the guidelines for permanence and durability of the Committee on Production Guidelines for Book Longevity of the Council on Library Resources and the minimum requirements of the American National Standard for Permanence of Paper for Printed Library Materials Z39.48-1984.

Library of Congress Cataloging-in-Publication Data
Oates, David, 1950-
 City limits : walking Portland's boundary / David Oates ; with contributions from William Ashworth ... [et al.].-- 1st ed.
    p. cm.
 Includes bibliographical references and index.
 ISBN-13: 978-0-87071-095-7 (alk. paper)
 ISBN-10: 0-87071-095-8 (alk. paper)
 1. City planning--Oregon--Portland Metropolitan Area. 2. Regional planning--Oregon--Portland Metropolitan Area. 3.   Cities and towns--Oregon--Portland Metropolitan Area--Growth. 4.   Greenways--Oregon--Portland Metropolitan Area. 5. Open spaces--Oregon--Portland Metropolitan Area. I. Title.
 HT168.P67O37 2006
 307.1'21609795'49--dc22   2005035973

3451 5360 12/06

Oregon State University Press
500 Kerr Administration
Corvallis OR 97331-2122
541-737-3166 • fax 541-737-3170
http://oregonstate.edu/dept/press

"Everything that is useful to the whole business of living together in a civilized way is energy well spent."
—Italo Calvino

"Without community, we are all doomed to private worlds that are more selfish and loveless than they need to be."
—Douglas S. Kelbaugh

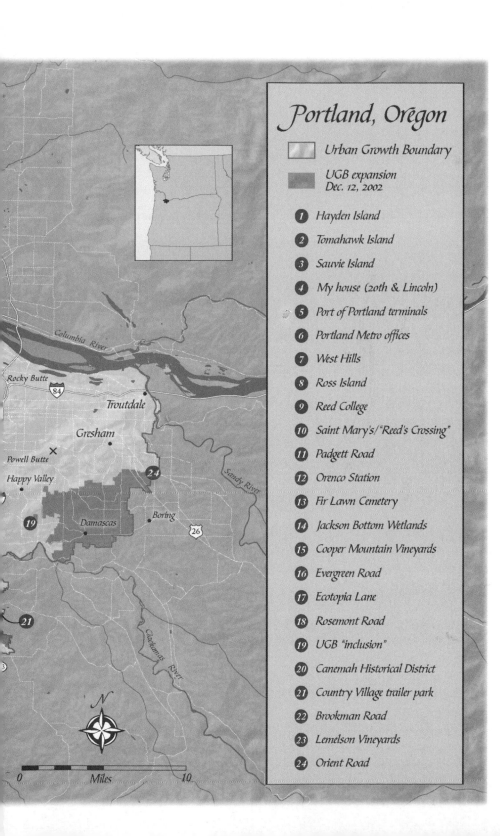

Portland, Oregon

- Urban Growth Boundary
- UGB expansion Dec. 12, 2002

1. Hayden Island
2. Tomahawk Island
3. Sauvie Island
4. My house (20th & Lincoln)
5. Port of Portland terminals
6. Portland Metro offices
7. West Hills
8. Ross Island
9. Reed College
10. Saint Mary's/"Reed's Crossing"
11. Padgett Road
12. Orenco Station
13. Fir Lawn Cemetery
14. Jackson Bottom Wetlands
15. Cooper Mountain Vineyards
16. Evergreen Road
17. Ecotopia Lane
18. Rosemont Road
19. UGB "inclusion"
20. Canemah Historical District
21. Country Village trailer park
22. Brookman Road
23. Lemelson Vineyards
24. Orient Road

Contents

Introduction: Where I Walked, What I Walked For 1

Distance from the Center 6

   William Ashworth, "Monopoly Money" 14

   Ana Maria Spagna, "A View from Teensy Town" 18

The John Muir Reappearances 26

Boots on the Ground in Sherwood Forest 32

   David Bragdon, "Inside Out" 39

   Kelly Rodgers, "Dialogue: The Neglect of 'Here' " 42

Seemingly Paul Shepard 47

City Limits 52

   Holly Iburg and Gary Conkling, "Reed's Crossing" 62

   Kathleen Dean Moore, "Boundaries" 67

Doublewides in Ecotopia 71

   David Hassin, "Walking the Line" 80

Italo Calvino Invisibly 84

   Eric Lemelson, "The View from a Vineyard" 91

Epilogue: A Democracy of Water 96

Notes 106

Works Cited 119

Index 124

Acknowledgments

This was a collaborative trek, and I have the pleasure of thanking many who walked, talked, encouraged, and helped.

Thanks be unto:

Every driver who missed me on the side of the road.

Folks along the way who chatted, offered water, let me use their phones.

My fellow walkers and kayakers, who offered time and companionship that I relished and learned from, and who creatively turned their experiences into chapters for this book.

Other friends who walked or paddled with me: Courtney Frisse and Tim Tidyman-Jones in boats; Gale Robinson, Steve Karakashian, Horatio Law, Jason King, Roger Dorband, and Meg Rowe on foot.

Helpful people in many offices of local and regional government who willingly offered information, advice, and direction: Karen Scott Lowthian, Carol Hall, and the other knowledgable people at Metro's Data Resource Center; Michael Tomsovic, Portland Office of Transportation; Laura Hudson and Bryan Snodgrass, both of the City of Vancouver Long Range Planning Department; Diana Cornelius, Seattle City Demographer; and Ted Winter, Port of Portland Facility Engineer, Marine Terminals, who took me on a tour of riverfront port facilities.

Reference librarians (and friends) at Clark College's Cannell Library, Tao Schmidt and Joan Carey, who responded quickly and creatively to my many demands; and the anonymous but instantaneously helpful online Multnomah County Reference Librarians; my good friend Ian Simpson who regularly pointed me toward answers for legal questions; and Dr. Laurel J. Standley of Watershed Solutions LLC (Portland) for help with assessing the economic and ecological values of wetlands.

Mary Elizabeth Braun, Acquisition Editor at OSU Press, for her steady encouragement and shaping advice as the project unfolded.

And thanks also to the men and women who fought—and cooperated!— to make Portland a remarkable community in a remarkable state: political leaders and anonymous neighborhood participants alike. Every Oregonian owes you a debt of gratitude, and a responsibility to add our own collective rebuilding energies to the project of living together.

Introduction

Where I Walked, What I Walked For

I walked all the way around Portland, along the invisible line called the Urban Growth Boundary. Where the dotted line followed rivers—the Sandy, the Clackamas, the Willamette, the Columbia—I went in a kayak. But it was mostly just a long walk on city streets and rural two-lanes. Once in a while I could bushwhack across fields or hilltops when the boundary didn't follow the road; otherwise I approximated its zigzags and doglegs, taking the nearest walkable route. I journeyed intermittently for two years and two months.

There were many interruptions. A war was declared. I had knee surgery. I sent a pair of books to press and taught courses. The boundary itself shifted and pulsed like a living thing. I tried to walk the map . . . and of course found that the territory did not cooperate. Somewhere between the map and the territory was Portland, that dream of a good place to live. I wandered along the boundary, sometimes inside, sometimes out, often lost in the gap between intention and execution, utopia and reality.

That's what walking is for. Experience that closes the gap—or gets productively lost in it.

◆

I wanted to give my legs a chance to think. I seem smarter when I'm moving, as if a day's walk expanded my mind—legs the smartest; then the spine loosening and the lungs filling; eventually even the head, that fourteen pounds of wet busyness adding its bit of memory or language, then finally the whole range of vision becoming a presence, a delicate external intellect. The topheavy bipedal miracle teeters confidently forward, thinking brave thoughts that start in the heel, arch to the toes, then blossom into the arc of a one-stride story, a tiny hopeful venture flying low and thudding finally home, its faith rewarded. In the safely grounded moment the next little leap is prepared. Maybe the next thought too.

Sometimes I walked with a friend at my side, and then I was smarter for sure. I enjoyed the strolling company of some select folks: an artist, writers, photographers, urbanists, environmentalists, developers, a politician, an agriculturalist. What they had to say about the experience is in this book too. I am grateful to each of them for their time and companionship and contribution.

Some were not literally alive at the time we walked (or ghost-walked) together. I took the liberty of writing up the imagined conversations myself. John Muir, Paul Shepard, and Italo Calvino came to me on my travels in seemings and emanations, spectres and memories of long hours spent with their books.

I passed by berryfields and vineyards and orchards along this perimeter: housing on one side and edens purloinable on the other! O taste and see, said the scriptures; so I did. This made me well-disposed toward the entire Urban Growth Boundary project, despite its lumbering superstructure of laws and bureaus, planners and land-use hearings, disputes and wrangles, and to oversee it all, an entire extra layer of government the like of which does not elsewhere exist in these United States, called "Metro" and hidden in plain sight in Northeast Portland.

It is a crazy, going-forward teeter of hopefulness, this Portland.

◆

As I walked and paddled and drifted, I wondered what my theme would be. After many days the obvious manifested: We were working out how—and whether—to live together.

I say "whether" because one answer is to live against each other, encapsulated behind walls of an illusory individualism. This delusion is now playing everywhere in America, and the consequences are ugly and frightening: seething resentment that seems to come from nowhere and to be directed everywhere, from a populace growing ever fatter, stupider, holier, and more ready to make war. That makes me sound cranky but sometimes it's good to tell the plain truth (these documented trends became all too visible while I walked). The know-nothing impulse to pull down, privatize, hoard one's pennies, mistrust everyone, and hole up has made another of its periodic reappearances in America.

The alternative is what this book turned out to be about: Portland's experiment in living with each other. Our Boundary, both visible border and invisible symbol, is our attempt to agree on how to live: what trade-offs to make so that all (not just a few) can benefit. Oregon's planning scheme is a bit of urban utopianism, an optimistic attempt to try and live a little better here in this blessed Northwest. As if people could ever agree! And yet they did. For more than thirty years, we agreed to see ourselves as a community, and to decide, collaboratively, what that meant.

Here's how it works. State law requires every municipality to cordon itself within a line on a map, the Urban Growth Boundary (or "UGB"). On the inside, homes and apartment-buildings and other kinds of urban development are planned and encouraged. Increased density is a goal. Good transit is a goal. On the outside, development and housing are discouraged or disallowed, "to preserve farms and forests" as the official UGB Website puts it. To administer the Portland area, Oregonians created an elected regional government (Metro) spanning three counties and twenty-four separate local entities. Every five years, Metro, accompanied by strenuous disagreeing and lawyering, must adjust the line outward according to detailed criteria, steering development away from the best natural or productive lands. A (supposed) twenty-year supply of developable land is required, so that growth is not stopped but channeled in ways shaped by communal design goals instead of individual profit. It is intended to manage growth, not limit growth. But as we will see, the actual application can be either (or neither).

By the time I finished walking it, the UGB extended 260 circumferential miles. Portlanders are highly aware of it. It's part of our identity. "Most progressive land-use laws in the nation," I've heard myself brag, usually to friends from California. Every so often our state's anti-government conservatives and developers try to undo the growth-boundary idea, but it has lasted since the initial statewide law was passed in 1973 creating a state Land Conservation and Development Commission (LCDC) with a mandate to keep cities from sprawling into farms and forests. Until recently, at least, the system has not only endured, it has prospered. Planners from around the country—and the world—come to study it, and they habitually refer to it as an example of how the "New Urbanism" works. It has given Portland a pleasant and dynamic downtown, close-in neighborhoods that folks love to live in, pretty good public transit, and a fighting chance not to spread endlessly, meaninglessly, in every direction. We think the orchards, fields, and vineyards of the Willamette Valley that have not been covered by tract housing will continue to make our lives richer. We hope to grow in and, in places, up. To become richer in connections and cleverness—to get deeper—instead of wider, flatter, and shallower.

In other words, our border makes us smarter, somehow. It gives us the means to think about ourselves. We know where we end, who's next to us. Like when we take a walk, we feel ourselves a little more in focus.

Until recently, anyway. Like all utopias, it could be about to vanish (by a statewide vote taken shortly after I finished walking—discussed in the Epilogue). Shouldn't surprise anyone. The fun will be to see if we can pull off another miracle, another little flight of hope, and reconfigure our hopeful community yet again.

◆

I went light on my journey, unread in the voluminous literature of urbs and suburbs, architecture and planning and design. I wanted to see fresh what was there. Much later, as the project took shape by foot and I began to fill in the reading, I felt surprised to find my approach prefigured in Lucy Lippard's *Lure of the Local*: "One way to find ourselves is to walk the map, to think about how the land around us is being and has been used. Looking at land through nonexpert eyes, we can learn a lot." That was the faith I started with—that open eyes and an open mind could figure some things out and bring a report.

And when I ran across James Howard Kunstler's jeremiad against the suburbanization of America, *The Geography of Nowhere*, it struck me right away that his "nowhere" is a sort of back-translation of that older, more starry-eyed term "utopia" (*a-topos* = no place). Perhaps "nowhere" is what's left when utopia evaporates. America was founded by utopian dreamers, whose hearts rose into their throats as they planned and built their escapes, their theocracies, their republics, their cities-on-the-hill. So it is no slight when I claim this high ground for Portland. Douglas Kelbaugh, a modern master of the urban question, has written that all the theory and blueprints in the world mean little, in the achieving of a real city, without those invisible ingredients I thought about most often during my walk: that certain idealism, naive perhaps, that yearning and striving he names, from the Greek, *arete*. Portland's civic humanism has been a powerful force. Why has it arisen here and not elsewhere? What is the music that builds our city?

One answer arose many months later, while I was walking in a semirural part of Southwest Portland. It seemed like the kernel of this whole experience.

On that day, when I turned to walk up SW Grabhorn, I got a sort of urban vertigo, a city/country confusion. On the supposedly "city" side, the spring-green rows of a large vineyard covered a hill, with a set of buildings nestled near the top that could only mean one thing: Tasting Room. The sign announced Cooper Mountain Vineyards. A bucolic oasis—except that oversized newer housing crowded to the very edges of the sloping vineyards. Inside or outside the UGB? It was a hot day and I was glad, after climbing the hill, to step into the cool interior, where a cluster of friendly, heavyweight visitors from the Midwest were tasting.

Behind the bar was Morgan, an attractive young woman briskly pouring out free samples, because of . . . what was it? Some kind of special day. My timing was perfect. As I sipped whites and then reds and then a white again, Morgan told me about her family farm, not far south on Bull Mountain, which went back to pioneer days. Her great-grandfather (a man named Harris) had been wagonmaster of an overland party, and he had staked out the farm on arriving in the Oregon utopia.

Perfect, I thought: Here is the daughter of wandering pioneers, learning the settled-in art of viniculture. Growing grapes, making wine: It's an art of place. The French word for it, a wine-drinking word, is *terroir*. That means: the qualities that are here and nowhere else. What you know when you pay attention. What you care about when you decide to stay and make a life here, here, with no safety valve of just clearing out when problems arise, grabbing the quick profits and heading further west. There is no west from here. This is it.

That's the music that builds this place—what we hear when we listen to land and river and each other—what creates that transcendent terroir called community.

Yet (to finish the episode) I also saw signs advertising a subdivision standing right out among the grape trellises. Morgan said the vineyard was to be sold; the owner had some other vineyard acreage, safe outside the UGB, to which he would transfer the winemaking operation. The crowding suburbs would win. Pity, I thought. I was particularly enjoying the Reserve Chardonnay, which started simply with a nice citrus crispness but then mellowed to a surprising buttery afterglow in the mouth. It put me in the mood to forgive. Let the vineyard move if it must. If we can keep the UGB in place, perhaps it won't have to move again.

Distance from the Center

This morning I have parked my car and walked to the crest of rolling SE 147th Avenue. In a half hour's stroll I have seen fancy farms and ranchettes on pretty uplands, forests and vineyards and green fields of pastoral bliss. And also one densely overbuilt tract of suburban housing.

My plan is to walk Portland's Urban Growth Boundary, all of it. It's late June; it will be hotter later. I'm glad to have gotten started. By the end of today I will have marched ten miles on or near the thick purple dotted UGB line on my map, approximating the legal boundary along rural and suburban streets and following it precisely across one mile of tallgrass field, burrs in my socks and scratches on my legs and rock-rose islands big as Cadillacs to find my way around. I'll walk counterclockwise, northeasterly, and end up almost in Gresham.

Since the inception of Oregon's land-use system in the 1970s, Portland has evolved from a decaying, lackluster provincial burg, into one of the nation's most successful and distinctive cities. One of the things I'd like to figure out, as I walk, is whether the UGB might be contributing to that success. And if so, how.

Too much, alas, for one day's walk. . . . Maybe I'll be wiser in a year or so, when I've finished the whole thing.

A boundary is a lie that reveals truths. Sharp edges—distinctions—are indispensable to clear thinking. On a map, the UGB looks perfectly clear. It says we are separate. But in fact we are connected.

◆

So here I am on 147th, turning my head to see the fullness of suburban-ization cramming the valley-bottom below me—that seething development we all depend on and fear, stimulate and hold back. I gaze down onto hundreds of shingled roofs, inflatable pools, garages. The houses are too big for their lots. Twenty years ago these broad-shouldered two-storys would have been above-average-sized houses, but now they are tract-standard, their five-foot side setbacks making intimates of neighbors. I guess people want a lot of square footage for their money so there it is.

This place is called "Happy Valley." I'm not kidding.

Happy Valley. It's just too easy, isn't it? Yet—are they really to blame for wanting to be happy?

And next door to it: "Pleasant Valley." And next to that: "Pleasant Valley Cemetery." Deaf to irony, these glad-handed salesmen and innocent homebuyers. Oh, c'mon, I tell myself, don't be so judgmental. Folks with families to raise—who could blame them? It's the most they can find in the Portland area for the money. *Happy Valley, Psychotic Valley, whatever. Just get me a place for this family.* People doing their best.

That leaves me, on foot out on the roadway, looking on. What gives me the right to mock? I have no kids and don't want 'em—I live with my guy just off Hawthorne, a nice close-in neighborhood, and to me city life in Portland is the best of everything: a quiet room where I can write; a vibrant city just out my door where I can recharge myself. Enough solitude, enough company; other folks' thoughts and creativities surging all around me: My formula for reasonable happiness.

Aren't you lonely out here? I want to ask those suburbanites. A tiny bit bored? Happy Valley is exactly the sort of thing the UGB is designed to corral, isn't it?—to prevent the entirety of Oregon from 82nd Avenue to Mt. Hood and from Beaverton to Cannon Beach from turning into suburbs like this. Maybe I'm not the only one who thinks they are not, after all, such a wonderful life-form.

Soon I'm walking up the hilly dead-end of 145th. I'll have to backtrack later but I want to see how the UGB runs along the wooded hilltop just behind these houses. When I go up a cutbank to look close, I see second-growth Douglas-fir crowding its whole other life right up to the magic line. For one morning hour, this vivid parallel world hovers above the street. To look up and see it releases a surprising contentment in me. All's well, tucked under a hill and a forest, with a view to keep watch. The human habitat, maybe, imprinted deep in an old part of the brain. Edge of the forest. Safety and a prospect of possible dangers, or dinners.

Maybe that is why this street, on higher ground overlooking the happy housing below, features larger houses. "Mansionettes" is the real-estate word. Just here, for instance: twin Corinthian columns flanking a front door totally out of proportion with the house, dwarfing everything except the owner's self-importance. But a little further on a neighbor has topped this display with four columns—Ionic this time, equally silly. *Ranch-Parthenon,* the sales agent might say. *Very popular.* Behind the columns I can see a big generic entry hall; above them, fake-slate roof; around them, detailing that looks manufactured and tired despite the fact I probably couldn't afford it. Sleek, bland, and upper-middle; identical in style, if not in scale, to hundreds of other houses visible from this very driveway . . . plus the columns.

Bourgeois folly. I'm no Flaubert and I cannot do it justice. Somehow I just don't enjoy pot-shotting these earnestly presumptuous Republicans (I've seen their bumperstickers). Houses like these are self-satirizing. What need for me to do it?

◆

It's striking how far from any center I feel, out here amidst the middle-class lawns and garages. I'm jumpy, ill-at-ease, fearful even. Although I grew up in suburbs, I never feel comfortable there. Or maybe it's *because* that's where I grew up, in the ranch-style anomie of greater Los Angeles, those spaces of endless one-story houses connected by streets without sidewalks leading to boulevards that go on for miles without any distinguishing feature or relishable moment: supermarket, parking, used-car, fast food, supermarket, parking. Wandering in LA or Houston or Phoenix, one place could pretty much be any place. No center, no circumference, no meaningful detail in between.

Distance from the center is what I'm thinking about as I walk this hot, intermittently thoughtful day. A phrase that seems to bring these issues into focus.

If a boundary is a skin, a limit, a way to distinguish self from not-self, then the UGB seems like a way for a newish western town to assert that it indeed has an identity: that it knows where it ends and what it is. "Distance from the center" implies that one place has a relation to other places: to the center first of all, the place of convergence, and also to the edge where intensities relax and then, distinctly, cease. You can map any point by reference to center and circumference, metering the intensity, knowing where you're at: Edge or Downtown or in between.

"Distance from the center" implies meaning, in other words: some way to triangulate the details with the big picture. That's what I crave: meaningful places. No one like a convert—poor li'l LA boy, I'm a big fan, an aficionado, of this Portland thing because it offers me an alternative to the dilute life of the endless suburbs.

I feel an emotional scaling on this meter. At the intense center there is enrichment. But there is also possible entrapment. That's the downside— what my rural pals are thinking when they roll their eyes about Big City: all that noise, all those people, gahh, how do you stand it . . .

And at the edge, of course, along with peaceable solitude, that room for nesting families, there is the possibility of loneliness. Isolation, disconnection.

So "distance from the center" is the physical and emotional yardstick of a place that is a place. Its center and its edge are located, findable. And feelable, too: each has its paradoxical human meanings marked out as well. Emotional trade-offs, clarified by their relation to each other: This, not that. More connected (but crowded); more private (but isolated).

◆

Along the country road called Butler, I walk through a fabulous green dell: lacy locust canopy, thickets of blossoming blackberries, tall swaying foxglove spikes. A little further on, I make good time in alder-shade above a little creek. Aside from the occasional car or truck rushing past on the two-lane, the effect is charming, restoring.

But when the pickups whiz by, I feel vulnerable and out of place, a little afraid of guys in country pickups. I'm a goofball with skinny legs walking . . . walking? Why's he walking?? It takes so little to not-fit-in out here. And what I know about these communities, both tract-suburban and semi-rural, is that they're fundamentally tribal. They're good to each other. If you move there and go to their church, they're the best neighbor, helper, friend in the world. None better, anywhere. But you must belong to the clan.

And if you don't, god help you.

I suppose these suburbs express American individualism. Me, my immediate friends; everyone else can go jump. Tax-revolt fundamentalism. Spiritual and political individualism.

But "distance from the center" works on a different theory. It presupposes there is a shared identity. An "us." This alone creates a difference from the Houston/LA/Mexico City pattern of endless amorphousness, each citizen on his or her own. In Portland, we are making a stand against it. "Don't Californicate Oregon" wins all arguments here, at least so far.

For the Portland theory is that people are not isolated individuals, despite the national Marlboro-man ideology. And I buy this communalism completely. We are webbed in to each other; almost everything important comes to us through the cooperative goodwill of literally uncountable other folks, past and present. We cannot think a thought, speak our native tongue, drive down the street, or even stand there in our genes except by profound connectedness to the other humans who have built the species for a million years, body and mind, and who are doing so this very moment all around us. What we receive from others is, pretty much, everything. This implies reciprocal responsibility. And it gives, in return, opportunity for an expanded soul, a self that includes others: that infinite filigree of loves and friendships and affinities that give the solitary journey its joy. Libertarian individualism has had to overlook almost everything real and everything delicious about our human lives, in order to sustain its lone-wolf illusion.

I suppose, as a writer and a teacher, I know this reality with particular vividness. My work, day by day, is directed to it, and draws from it. To read is to become intimates with other minds, transgressing limits of space and time and body. To write or teach is to insist on the clarifying disciplined mutuality of shared language and exploration. When the National Endowment for the Arts conducted its study of American reading habits— and found literary reading on the decline, with less than half of Americans now bothering to read a book—poet and NEA Chair Dana Gioia made the application to civic connectedness explicit. "Reading develops a capacity for focused attention and imaginative growth that enriches both private and public life." Readers, he said, "are nearly three times as likely to attend a performing arts event, almost four times as likely to visit an art museum, more than two-and-a-half times as likely to do volunteer or charity work. . . . People who read more books tend to have the highest level of participation in other activities." It is true for all our arts and celebrations. What is a polished Brancusi, a Mozart sonata, a crowded hip-hop dance floor, but a reaching out from some shared place? "Only connect," says Forster.

And cities, with their measured intensities center to edge, their play of possibility, express that connectedness. Our Boundary, marking us off in one way, in another way expresses a touching and surprising solidarity within that Boundary. We think we are "we," a community that can make decisions about itself: a whole, not just a blind statistical aggregate. We think we can see ourselves in this odd-shaped mirror with a purple dotted line around it.

SUVs and pickups whiz by on the country highway. I stay way over on the shoulder. Out here, I'm a bug on the grille. Not much more.

At last I arrive at the landscaped edge of Persimmon Country Club Community. ("Community, hah," I mutter.) I use my borrowed cell-phone to call a Green Cab, and in the twenty minutes it takes the taxi to find me I unlace my boots and finish my last water bottle, wondering what difference that line on a map, corralling growth inside its legal limit, has made. And feeling a very long distance from the center.

◆

But instead of going straight home to shower off the day's sunblock, I find myself walking up a little wooded mountain. When the taxi lets me off by my car, I cannot resist the chance to be both inside and outside the border of our town—at the same time. For this rustic hilltop is marked out on the map as an exclusion (or is it an inclusion?), a rural island completely surrounded by urb. Here the Boundary actually defines an inside edge; here it is "nature" that's enclosed and "city" that's all around. It makes me think of the yin-yang symbol, with its dot of oppositeness on each side of the wavy line. It makes me think of the organism/environment boundary, which gets vaguer and vaguer the more you look at it: since, as Alan Watts says, your skin, marking your outside, is equally the universe's skin, marking its inside. So whose boundary is it?

Just downhill are glimpses of Happy Valley, not far from where I began. But up here it's all forest, that soft wind-in-the-branches sound in dappled light. It's a surprising moment, here inside the UGB, even bit wildernessy, though I can see a couple of nice houses under the towering Doug-firs, each with acreage and roadside mailbox, and beyond them a line-up of mailboxes down a dirt road. Still, it seems more like mountain resort than suburb.

I said that the UGB helps define Portland's identity. But identity itself is shifty, isn't it? Ecologically, all places are connected. Economically, the life of Oregon flows into and out of Portland with little regard for the UGB. What's the line mean, after all? What's inside, what's out?

In fact—to enrich the question—I later found out that the entire stretch I hiked that first day was destined to transform from edge to interior. The new maps had not yet been published, but decisions had been taken to move the whole Urban Growth Boundary far south to Damascus and Boring. All the edge effects I saw on this first day will be transferred out there. Metro has to redraw the UGB every five years to make room for orderly growth, but this is the largest expansion ever, some 18,700 acres (compared with, for instance, the 1998 expansion of 3,500 acres).

So the crisp, clear definitions of the UGB give way, in the end, to more questions. Is this just sprawl after all, though under a different name? Is this thing working? If a boundary is a lie, it ought at least to be a useful one. At the end of ten miles in suburbia and one mile in a never-land of woods, with occasional glimpses of the gleaming center, I wonder how to assess that.

Coda

Driving home in a cloud of thought and then sitting late to type my notes, it occurs to me that Portland could be riding that paradox of boundaries in a most productive way. "Distance from the center" works for us. Here's how: By making Portland a center in its own right, we can be inside and outside at the same time.

That's something you simply cannot do in DC, NY, or LA. They are global centers, their gravitational pull inescapable and ravenous. Though they do end, they have no meaningful edges; and nothing escapes their black-hole power sink. All center, no edge, they fall fully into their own illusion of omnipotence, dazzled by their own glamor. The city-lie: Babylon, Pandemonium. It's as if the world around them has ceased to exist.

At the other extreme, there's no sense of center at all when you're in Fargo or Modesto or Bakersfield. Folks there have chosen to live off the grid, in places which have only flimsy human mapping. However rewarding the private life there might be, they have to draw their sense of the expansive human drama from somewhere else. Off the edge, lost in whatevery anywhereness, they consume the news and movies and books that come from elsewhere.

But here in the right-sized provincial capital, perhaps we can have both. We are far enough from the global/galactic powercore to make our own core valuable and interesting. When we insist on identity, on a real edge and a meaningful center, it works partly because of this luck of continental placement: just-separate-enough. Take a look at a map, and consider the outsized historical importance of those two little islands of Britain and Japan. For most of their histories, they were far enough from continental powers and upheavals to develop their own unique cultures, yet close enough to receive regular infusions of ideas and cultural wake-ups. Distance from the center, calibrated just right.

That is Portland's geographic gift. Not quite on the coast, yet a seaport. Grain terminus for the Great Basin, yet looking out over the Pacific Rim. Three hours from Seattle, who knows how far from California . . . where is Portland, exactly? No one who's not from here could find us on a map. Portland instinctively grasps this point and builds an urban ethos around it: our tendency to mute our presence on the national scene. Writers from

William Stafford onwards have noticed this hiding-in-plain-sight habit. We are a sort of secret. We don't really want big-league teams and all that attention. We don't mind if Seattle, San Francisco, and LA hog the limelight. Let 'em. We'll be up here living well: small enough to look over our Boundary and enjoy our mountains and forests; big enough to stay in town and be nourished.

Ah, but it's just Portland, poor little provincial Puddletown? I answer: Real provinciality—the provincialism of snobs and wannabes—is the Bovaristic feeling that something better and realer must be going on somewhere else. At our best we know it ain't so: it's here. I've walked the galleries of New York, Paris, London; sat in the Concertgebouw and the Staatsoperhaus. I read the books. The real thing is here, whether those self-involved global centers choose to know it or not. It's here in smaller quantities, to be sure. And there can be a preciousness about it at moments. . . . But then there's a groundless, inflated self-importance in New York arts and artifacts that comes to the same thing. Good work appears, in about the same measure, in both places. Oh, that sounds like booster bravado . . . until you listen compositions by Tomas Svoboda or Brian Johanson (or Pink Martini!), read a LeGuin or a Spanbauer, take a look at a Stephen Hayes or Michael Brophy landscape, or lose yourself in the dance of Minh Tran or Body Vox (or Linda K. Johnson, who danced right on the Boundary a few years back). They are the real thing.

And few places, large or small, have a more developed civic ethic than Portland: that passionate, paying-attention citizenry. City Club of Portland is only its best-known manifestation. Groups abound for riverkeeping and urban-repairing and bicycling and putting lights on bridges . . . on top of the formal city-government structure that includes funded Neighborhood Associations. We are an urban populace that notices, that cares about getting it right, that shows up, that makes noise until the politicians respond.

Portland may be building a place—just far enough away, just close enough—where meaningful edges and a defined center give us groundedness in place and expansiveness of spirit. That's our civic goal, our Portland commitment, argued and plotted endlessly: the good place, under the watchful view of snowy Mt. Hood, where we work on being human together.

WILLIAM ASHWORTH is a retired librarian who also writes nonfiction books (twelve to date, all on natural history and environmental topics). A founder of the Oregon Chapter of the Sierra Club and longtime member of the chapter's executive committee, he left the club over disagreements about environmental stewardship versus preservation. His book on this topic, *The Left Hand of Eden,* won the Oregon Book Award in 1999.

Bill and his wife Melody were game to explore a somewhat loopy section of far-eastern UGB, out along country roads and a bit of Springwater Corridor trail. We marched up and down dirt roads beside a strange mixture of nice country homes and sloppy rural messes where Faulkner might have looked for Snopeses. The UGB was not particularly accomodating that day. We were right on it at first, but then it just took off over a woodsy hill. We kept telling each other, "It's over there somewhere." But these two had sharp eyes for plants and birds and they were willing walkers. We ended up making about eight miles, circling that woodsy hill.

Monopoly Money

William Ashworth

The elderly pickup was doing fifty miles per hour—barely—in the right-hand lane of Interstate 5. It was small and yellow and had seen better millennia, and although it looked clean and lovingly cared for, fifty miles per hour was probably as fast as its driver dared to take it. As my wife dashed us past, I read the homemade warning sticker glued to the back of the pickup's cab. It said, "It is illegal to operate this equipment."

We had spent the earlier part of this cool September day near Boring, in the southeast part of the Portland metropolitan area, walking part of the Urban Growth Boundary with David. The sky was a watery gray that never quite delivered on its threat; the transparent air gave us a sweep of view that reached all the way to Larch Mountain, tucking its head into the cloudy ceiling sixteen airline miles away. There was a rustle and whisper of Fall. An orderly dance of young red maples along Country Club Road was just beginning to blush scarlet. My biologist wife amused herself by identifying the animals that had been flattened into the pavement by passing traffic. A weasel. Several red squirrels. A frog, in two parts, fresh enough that its spilled intestines still glistened damply with digestive fluids. I watched a woolly bear caterpillar waddle onto the pavement of SE 242nd Avenue, headed innocently for the far side, almost certain to become a smudge on a fast-moving tire before it could get there.

This part of the UGB is oddly shaped. Actually, all of its parts are oddly shaped: its course follows rules only a city planner could love. East-west roads. North-south roads. Portions of gravel lanes. Rivers, creeks, and rivulets. Beeline cross-country runs that are not quite beelines, but jog carefully back and forth along property boundaries, as if the bees were reading tiny little No Trespassing signs. David led us as close to this conundrum as he could, sometimes walking directly on it, sometimes paralleling it at a distance, backtracking where necessary, covering nearly eight miles of pavement, gravel, and turf in order to view two miles of mapped line. It was not very efficient, but it got the job done.

Like the UGB itself. It is not very efficient, but it gets the job done. You might not want to drive it more than fifty miles per hour in the right-hand lane, but it will take you to your destination. The night before, Melody and I had joined David for dinner at a brewpub in the Hawthorne District, one of Portland's burgeoning civic neighborhoods. The scene was lively, cosmopolitan, and still safe enough to walk the mile from David's house to it and back again after dark. A variety of causes contribute to Portland's liveability, but the UGB is certainly one of them. It does this by controlling density. Enough people to provide business for brewpubs; enough elbow room to avoid agoraphobia. Distances that encourage you to walk and other walkers that don't frighten you out of it. These things might happen without the discipline of the UGB, but they seem unlikely. Elsewhere, growth follows the rules of Monopoly. Snap up Boardwalk and Park Place and force the other players out of the game. Buy low; sell high. And because the edge of the city is where you can buy low and the center is where you can sell high, the result, inevitably, is a ringworm scar of decay. The edge sprawls out and the center builds up, and what is neither edge nor center has no place to go but downhill. The UGB prevents the edge from sprawling, stopping the whole dynamic in its Gucci tracks. Development rebounds into the part of the urban area that is neither edge nor center; the downhill slide reverses. The Hawthorne District and its many brethren are the pleasant result.

But this pleasantness does not come without costs. Boundaries have side effects. John Muir was right: when you try to pick out anything by itself, you find it attached to everything else in the Universe. Boundaries do not sever these attachments, they merely make them painful. The part of the boundary that we walked with David was recently redrawn, so the pain is not yet apparent. But it will arrive. Property inside the boundary will escalate in value against property outside. The lucky players will stack up their piles of Monopoly money and retire from the board; the rest will be stuck with the result. The result will include open space and wildlife outside and liveable neighborhoods inside, and that is some compensation. But the costs of maintaining these things are not borne equally. We all enjoy them. We do not all have to watch our next-door neighbors sell their land to developers for mucho dinero while we cannot.

Money isn't everything. It is much easier to mouth that cliché when it is not your money you are talking about.

And the boundary does not prevent all environmental problems—or even very many of them. It may control humans, but it is utterly transparent to natural forces. In an unnamed creek bottom draining into Johnson Creek, the three of us admired a lavish profusion of orange flowers that Melody identified, tentatively, as jewelweed. We keyed the plant out later. She was right—but no guidebook we were able to find recognized its existence west of Nebraska. Jewelweed is a foreign invader and, from the look of the patch we saw, quite capable of blitzkrieg. David had wondered at the juxtaposition of the contrary terms "jewel" and "weed" in the plant's name. Its beauty is clearly responsible for the first part. We are likely to find out about the second part considerably sooner than we care to. For this, the presence of the UGB will make no bloody difference whatsoever.

Boundaries are useless. They are also required. They do not work, but for some tasks they are the only things that work at all.

The day warmed as we proceeded. Overshirts came off. The sun brightened the damp woods. A mouse huddled on a cutbank, still as a mouse, trying to make itself invisible. A northern harrier circled above a field, perhaps seeking the mouse's cousin, perhaps simply trying to catch an updraft. We were circling, too, coming around by roads east of the boundary to the car parked at our starting point, a small eddy on the large circular stream that is the UGB—this inscrutable, blunt, impossible, and necessary instrument that bestows on Portland debates and brewpubs, harriers and unharried neighborhoods, fiscal inequalities and one of the nation's best urban qualities of life. Watch out for woolly bears. Keep your eye on the traffic and the jewelweed. Go directly to jail, do not pass GO, do not collect two hundred dollars.

When you try to pick out a brewpub by itself, you find it attached to everything else in the Universe.

Money isn't everything. Isn't everything money? Everything isn't money.

It is illegal to operate this equipment.

ANA MARIA SPAGNA lives and works in Stehekin, Washington, located at the roadless northern end of long, fjord-like Lake Chelan. Her short stories and essays have appeared in *Orion, Oregon Quarterly, Fine Homebuilding, Best Essays NW*, and *Stories From Where We Live: Northwest Pacific Coast*. Her first book, *Now Go Home: Wilderness, Belonging, and the Crosscut Saw*, appeared in 2004 from Oregon State University Press. She was raised in Southern California.

◆

Ana Maria and I had planned this walk since I visited her the previous summer, when we sat together talking beside the lake while snow-covered North Cascades peaks went rosy in the twilight and then faded to dark silhouettes beneath the stars. I admired her life there, so far from everywhere, though I knew I could never choose it for myself. Our December walk, when it finally happened, helped me mark my official crossing of the Willamette. I was happy for company as I began the push westward, with perhaps a quarter of my journey behind me, and, in my mind, frighteningly suburban parts of Portland ahead.

A View from Teensy Town

Ana Maria Spagna

We zip our coats tight and pocket our hands as we head uphill from a small city park marking the confluence of rivers, conveniently right where the UGB crosses the Willamette and follows the Tualatin westwards. A cold rain is falling, and the Tualatin is running muddy brown, like hot chocolate froth, and I'm distracted. Water that color reminds me of a too-recent flood back home. Rain started in the night, and by midday, the whole wide valley raged like a stormy sea. As David and I walk, I can't help scanning the banks of the Tualatin River, gauging their stability, trying to determine where this river might choose first to gnaw, the way a new mother will keep one eye on a mischievous toddler. What will it be next? After witnessing a mountain river gobble acres of forest in one fell swoop, I can't help thinking that this stuff looks like fodder.

I should explain: I live, by choice and happenstance, in a teensy town in the North Cascades which is, by National Geographic reckoning, the most remote place in the lower forty-eight. That makes my perspective much the same, I'd imagine, as many would-be UGB supporters: we want either big city or big wilderness. All or nothing. Black or white. My perspective is just turned inside out (or, I should say, outside in)—most enviros live and work in the city and dream of when they can visit the wilderness, while I live and work in the wilderness and dream of when I can visit the city. Problem is, lately, when it comes to growth management laws, my record has been a tad dubious. So here I stand beside the Tualatin—the UGB for now—searching for shades of gray, trying my damnedest to ignore the muddy brown.

On the far side of the river, mossy alder and young Doug-fir grow in a lichen green tangle, the kind of nouveau-forest that makes visitors to the Northwest believe our forests are largely intact, the kind of forest that, in this climate, can grow back in the blink of an eye. For most of us, that much forest is, emotionally and aesthetically, enough. It's is pleasant to look at and peaceful to walk in. Ecology is, of course, another matter. Such a forest can be home to the opportunists, the easy adjustors, and the newcomers: mule deer, coyotes, raven, maybe even a bald eagle or two. Spotted owls or pine martens or cougars?—probably not.

This side of the river is crowded with very large, nearly identical, single-family homes with five-foot setbacks on either side. Two-car garages are mandatory, as are vinyl picture windows, sometimes semi-circular, separated by plastic sticks. The soggy real estate flyers which David checks, and occasionally pockets, put the average square footage at 2,500—just barely larger the national average of 2,300 for new homes, but considerably larger than the much-bandied-about 1970 average of 1,500.

"How big is enough?" I ask.

David shrugs. Not ours to answer, he seems to say, and of course he is right. On the setbacks, however, he's willing to weigh in.

"Only ten feet of space to muffle a fart," he says. "Not nearly enough."

I laugh, but I'm not feeling very amused. These houses bother me. If we're willing to accept Forest Enough—and, really, I am—how about House Enough?

It's a subject I've thought about a lot. Back home in the teensy town, people build their own homes with their own lumber, their own initiative, and often enough, with cash. What they build is, necessarily, small. Not one house in the valley is as large as these; few surpass that 1,500-square-foot benchmark. Without exception, what my neighbors build is clever and crafty, unfinished and unconventionally beautiful. There is the boat-builder who bends recycled beams in his living room to mirror a hull. A firefighter uses charred poles; a former seaman uses driftwood. Nearly everyone uses something, if not everything, salvaged. And their homes are built to last. The locally milled lumber is so tightly grained that you'll bend 16-penny nails into curlicues unless you pre-drill. If you don't have the trees, or if you want to keep them as such, you can search out reclaimed lumber that is equally solid. Of course here in Portland, closer to civilization—"the real world," some people call it—building codes would never allow most of those practices. Sometimes I think that the bureaucratic tangle assures mediocrity and greed the way strict parental rules can breed both blandness and rebellion. Then again, maybe I'm just being defensive.

Here's the story in a nutshell. For a decade, my partner Laurie and I worked seasonally as laborers. We lived in over twenty dwellings, most without indoor plumbing, and kept our possessions down to what could be packed semiannually into a Corolla. Neither of us wanted to make a sweeping life change—move to the city and take an office job, say—but we couldn't keep up with those moves. They were killing us. Problem was, in the teensy town, private land is hard to come by. Nearly eight hundred thousand acres of wilderness surround it; demand outstrips supply nearly a millionfold, and land values follow suit. The only way we could afford to buy a piece of property was to buy it with another couple, and—here comes the dirty word—subdivide. Growth management laws required a minimum lot size of 2.5 acres. Once surveyed, the property we bought was 4.89 acres. In order to subdivide, we had to apply for—and received—a variance. Hence the dubious past.

I fessed up to David early in our walk. "Of course, doing that went against everything I ever thought I'd believed," I said.

"How old are you?" David asked.

"Thirty-six," I answered.

"Right on time," he said, smiling.

His quick response reminded me of the time, a few years back, when I was preparing for a dinner party and asked George, a friend of mine in his late forties, whether he thought another mutual friend was vegetarian.

"She's twenty-three," George said with a shrug. "Everyone's a vegetarian when they're twenty-three."

And everyone, apparently, is a capitalist when they're thirty-six. Whether we buy groovy refurbished downtown condos or overhuge yardless megahomes, or we build cabins on the dregs of undeveloped woodlands, we take our preferred slice of American Pie. Ouch.

So now you see my true colors: I am full of very specific and personal ambivalences. I believe in wilderness, places untrammeled by humans, but my job, maintaining hiking trails, mainly consists of trammeling. I believe in growth management laws, but not, apparently, when they affect my plans. (Isn't there a difference, I want to say, between investment developments and scattered, brush-hidden, owner-built homes? Yes, yes, but ... I know the counterargument. It sounds like a refrain from the drug war: you may start small, but it inevitably leads to the hard stuff.) I believe in the UGB, but I look at these houses, and I think: you can have it. I want to scurry back to the woods, to my own personal subdivided paradise. The irony and hypocrisy are enough to drown my best intentions. I know. I know. I'm thirty-six. Right on time.

David and I follow the map's wandering boundary line out of a neighborhood and back beside the river, and I feel more at home here, under an overpass where pigeons coo then disperse. I pull off my glove to touch the water, not nearly as cold as the mountain water I'm used to, and I look across the way at a smallish home atop the hill. It's the kind of place that I think people like to see, simple and modest, surrounded by trademark rolling green hills, like Oregon fifty years ago, Oregon as it ought to be. The optimist in me with her keen new capitalist perspective thinks: well, at least those folks' property values must benefit from the UGB. The pessimist in me thinks the little place looks vulnerable, not just to development, when the UGB expands, but to the river. With me, today, it's One Thing Considered.

Nearly everyone in the teensy town lives in the floodplain, and we've had three major floods since 1990. Starting ten years ago, landowners began to get serious about protecting the banks: some riprap, some rootings from native plants, and mostly, bank barbs, triangles of placed boulders that jut out into the river, not meant to stop the current, but to slow it down. I was skeptical. I couldn't help but wonder if all the protections might just bump the river, pinball-style, to the opposite bank. I assumed that destruction, like development, would be of its own mind, running pell mell. (There were times, in fact, in the not-too-distant past when I would have cheered when a river jumped its banks, wreaking havoc indiscriminately, inevitably.)

But that's not what happened. After this last flood, except in the most precarious locations, the engineered protections worked. For the most part, places hard hit were undeveloped or not valued as highly, aesthetically or ecologically. For the most part, the work of a decade seems actually to have helped—not to prevent damage, mind you, but to mitigate it. Back here in Portland, I'm beginning to understand that perhaps that's precisely what the Urban Growth Boundary is supposed to do: slow development and also send it ricocheting pinball-style to some strategized locale, not to prevent development, but to perhaps mitigate the damage. Aesthetically and ecologically, I suppose it works pretty well. Emotions are another matter.

The river has become inaccessible, so David and I are left approximating a route to meet back up with the UGB, and something feels wrong. We are walking through a neighborhood on a Tuesday at three p.m., after-school hours, the hours which during my childhood would have flooded a gaggle of kids into the street, playing baseball or hide 'n' seek or run-through-the-sprinklers. The weather is poorer here, granted, than on my California cul de sac, but the indoor lights are off as well. The kids are at day care, I suppose, or maybe playing on sports teams. Or maybe, at an average price of $300,000, these homes are too pricey for a lot of families with kids. Whatever the reason, I am disconcerted, and not just because of nostalgia. Life in the teensy town, even midwinter, is hopping at three p.m. Kids are walking home from school, hauling sleds or skis. Adults are shoveling their porches or walking the dog, taking in what precious-little daylight they can. Even those who are working do so in plain view of everyone else, with us and among us. Extremes of geography funnel us together. We all live beside the river, the lone artery snaking between steep cliffy walls. And extremes of solitude cause us to reach out. At home, I spend the lion's share of my time maintaining connections to other people—attending potlucks and school functions (though I have no children of my own), throwing small dinner parties. And I'm not the only one. When mail arrives, just three times a week in winter, neighbors crowd the post office, ostensibly waiting for it to be distributed. I know it sounds funny coming from where I do, where the nearest grocery store is a two-hour boat trip away, but I find this too-quiet suburban afternoon almost unspeakably lonely. Creepy, even.

The flipside: I know plenty of people find my life strange, even creepy: no telephone lines, no TV reception, no grocery store, no tavern, not even a church. Though I grew up in suburbia, I live happily, charmed even, in the woods with the woman I love and an overfed cat, books and bikes and skis and a whole lot of open space. I can't help it if I think that's the key. Proximity to open space can make us, I think, more humble, more patient, sometimes even less greedy. On the morning after the flood, glacial silt coated the picturesque valley so thickly that it looked like the ruins of Pompeii. Water churned in the road bed and surrounded cabins as neighbors began to venture out, on foot, to survey the damage. And because we sit somewhat above the river, our house became a requisite coffee stop. Each of the neighbors had lost something: a bridge, a driveway, brand new carpet, a wood-fired hot tub, garden compost, or like us, a whole garden, but no one had been hurt, and the sun was coming out. Without fail, the coffee-drinkers were grateful for those none-too-small favors; they shrugged off the losses and pulled on waders and headed back out into the muck. Of course I realize that people everywhere pull up their proverbial bootstraps after a natural disaster. Maybe it's just easier to gracefully accept the setbacks and constraints dealt by Mother Nature than the ones offered by a committee of elected officials. Still, I'm thinking, even if the effects of the UGB on the inside of the line are not my cup of tea, there's always the outside.

David and I step off the asphalt and duck under a barbed wire fence, and pop out, unexpectedly, at a high point, a vista of sorts: Christmas tree farms and a strip mall. Between the two, not surprisingly, the UGB draws a tidy discernable line. The Christmas trees are closely spaced and radically pruned, and I try to gauge their age. Eight years or ten? Probably more. Here on the west side of the Cascades where the growing season is so long, I tend to underestimate. I'm happy to see that people have found the perfect niche, the perfect in-between, a way to make money on land that can't be paved over. Surely not with a hayfield, or a forest proper—a tree farm on an eighty-year rotation—but Christmas trees, sure. They mitigate nasty CO_2 omissions, and they (hopefully) make a fair profit, and they look, if not entirely natural, at least more so than the other side of the street, where a more predictable version of the American Dream is at work: Safeway, Starbucks, Hollywood Video. Here, where neon reds and greens light up the gloaming, I'm beginning to see shades of gray.

By four, darkness is threatening, and we have come to a bad stretch, a busy two- lane road with neither shoulders nor sidewalks that is, for now, the UGB. Cars have switched on their headlights, and we are walking directly into them. (At home, too, this is the most dangerous hour to walk on the road, because of the threat of cougars, who hunt at dusk.)

Before we reach our map-chosen destination, we decide to throw in the towel, and wander about finding a pay phone to call a cab to return us to the confluence where we left the car.

David notices a brightly Christmas-lit house on the other side of the busy road where Rudolph, Santa, and Frosty share the tiny front lawn.

"Those people will let us use their phone," David suggests.

We cross the street and enter a veritable Christmas bazaar. The open garage is lined with tables stocked with hundreds of trinkets: ornaments made of thread spools and clothespins and buttons, and mostly, ceramics. The woman who greets us, Viarda, must be nearly eighty. She sends her husband to phone a cab.

"Do you make any of these things?" David asks.

"I make all of them," Viarda replies. She's been doing it most of her adult life, first at craft fairs, then at home here in the garage that gets refitted each November to make room for the show. The ornaments are simple, and her daughter has taken over making most of them. The ceramics require more care. She buys the forms then paints and glazes and fires them herself in a kiln out back.

"That's a lot of work," I offer.

"Yes," she admits, "but I enjoy it."

When David asks, she says lived in this house for forty years. It used to be surrounded by farmland, and Viarda indulges us with a story of her young daughter and the horse she kept in the backyard.

"Couldn't keep one here now," she says. Her backyard is smallish and behind it, waves of houses rise unbroken toward the fading horizon. Out front traffic rushes on the two-lane road. Across the street is a dark open field. Just as the houses on the far side of the Tualatin are now more valuable, so too, perhaps, is Viarda's for its proximity to open space. We can only hope.

"More going in over here," she gestures right, "then real big ones down that way." She shakes her head regretfully, but reserves comment as if to say: Such is life.

David and I wander the aisles, wanting to buy something to repay her, both of us angling for whatever is the least Christmassy. Eventually, David chooses two ceramic mice with gigantic ears, and I select a set of snowy forest-painted mugs, and we hand over a few measly bills. Viarda's prices, like her stories and her work ethic, are firmly rooted in another era.

Viarda sighs. "I don't know if I'll do it next year," she says. "I just don't know if I can keep it up."

I don't buy it for a second. By the time the new year comes around, I'm pretty sure, she'll be back at it again, running her business out here in almost-country, remembering open fields while welcoming strangers in from the dark. When the cab arrives, David and I offer our thanks, and as we pull away, I gaze back at the red-tinted glow still emanating from the garage.

Here's what I'm thinking: we humans are astonishingly creative. Lines on the land can't decide or define or dictate how we live. If there's a way around the rule, we'll find it sure as salmon heading upstream. I found it myself. Guilty as charged. But here's what else I've decided: so what? Ambivalence itself is normal enough, a sign of flexibility, maybe even maturity. (It's the ugly twin offspring—anarchy and apathy—that cause all the trouble. Again I am, occasionally, guilty as charged.) That's where the UGB comes in, walking the ever-tenuous line. Not city or wilderness, but some kind of exurb verging on rurality. Not exactly my shade of gray, not exactly yours. Not this or that. Just a little more of this, and occasionally, a tiny hard-fought miracle: a little less of that.

The John Muir Reappearances

John Muir's white-bearded image, his extraordinary feats of endurance, potent advocacy for wilderness, and vivid depictions of wild places have shaped American attitudes about nature for well over a century.

Born in Scotland in 1838, Muir moved with his family to a farm in Wisconsin when he was ten years old. He studied botany and geology at the University of Wisconsin. After rambles on foot into Canada and all the way to Florida, Muir in 1869 took a job overseeing a herd of sheep in the California Sierra Nevada mountains, discovering in the process his home in Yosemite and his vocation as an interpreter and advocate. He spent two intense years hiking and climbing, forming a revolutionary theory of the role of glaciation that soon became accepted. He began writing nature-interpretation articles for the *San Francisco Bulletin* in the 1870s, travelling to Utah, Alaska, and the Northwest, lecturing, and meeting with luminaries such as Emerson on their visits to his mountains.

After an eight-year hiatus occasioned by his 1880 marriage to Louie Strentzel, family life with two children, and managing the Strentzel fruit ranch in Martinez, California, Muir returned to writing with a series of sketches from Oregon, Washington, and California. His 1890 articles for *The Century Magazine* led to the protection of Yosemite and struck a chord with a national audience. His most popular written work came out of extensive explorations in Alaska: "An Adventure With a Dog and a Glacier," later published as *Stickeen* (1909). He founded the Sierra Club in San Francisco in 1892, and continued traveling, writing, and preaching his "gospel of wilderness" until his death in 1914.

John Muir showed up on the day I started climbing into the West Hills from the tip of Sauvie Island. That's the northern end of Forest Park, and my attempt to follow the UGB there took me into deeply forested slopes. Ahead of me on the footpath I glimpsed a slight, wiry man with a grey beard but a young step. He stopped walking to let me catch up, and without a word we stood sociably with our heads tilted back, gazing into the dense Douglas-fir woods, the summer blue sky behind them, the slight sway of the treetops.

◆

JM: *"So beautiful, such bright-green drooping foliage! They grow so close together—you'd think it was a well-tilled field of grain."* He untilted his head. *"It's nice to be back."*

DO: "Yes. You stopped here in 1880. You gave some speeches."

"Talks. Lectures. Never speeches." His way was crisp, as if to cross him you'd be risking a sharp fight. *"Turn Halle. Natural Science Association. I spoke on glaciers. I was coming back from Alaska."*

"It was January. You got a couple paragraphs in *The Oregonian*. A nice little review."

He might have been pleased that I had read it, but he did not reveal much. "I saw some of the news in the same newspaper. There was a war in Afghanistan. The Democrats were disputing results of some elections; it was going to court. And Republican business was running the government."

"And? So what's the news about just now? I've been away, ye know ..."

"Well, it's ... it's exactly the same."

"Surely not exactly!"

"War in Afghanistan, only this time it's us, not the British. Democrats losing elections in the courts. Republicans and big business running the show in Washington. Same same."

We shrugged in unison. Bright bright summer light behind the trees seemed held up and away from us by the tall softness of sighing fir boughs. The antics of humans were nowhere in sight.

"And I was up in these wee hills before too, ye know," he said, playing the little Scots burr in his voice. *"South of here, with all Portland at our feet; a fine town, and both banks of the river in view ... sech a pretty river, full of leafy islands and willow banks."*

"So you've seen the layout here. These "wee hills" are the Tualatin Mountains ... the West Hills, we call them. They're like the spine. Everything connects to them. Visual reference point. Downtown, as you saw, nestles between them and the river. Over on the west side, Beaverton slopes off the other way, of course. But there to the east, you see it's a wide plain tipped toward the Willamette and kind of propped up, way out at the far edge, by little volcanic buttes and cones—Powell Butte, Rocky Butte. And Mt. Tabor's a tiny volcano, with a city park in the caldera!"

Suddenly Muir seemed interested. "I live over there, the soil's all clay, left here by tremendous scouring floods that came down the Columbia Gorge, end of the ice age."

"Volcanoes. Ice floods. Yes ... such desolation ... all for this, all for glorious far-reaching harmonies ... but such destruction ..."

He glanced over his shoulder to look out east where I gestured, since our upward path had entered a slight clearing. But something caught the corner of Muir's eye and turned him clean around to stare north. "What ... mountain ... is ... that?" he rasped, taken out of composure for the only time that I ever saw—or ever heard of, for that matter.

Then I understood. Muir, with his memory for detail and his love of mountains ... "Mount St. Helens," I offered quietly, watching to see the reaction.

"But ... when ...?"

"About twenty-five years ago. Blew off thirteen hundred feet. I climbed it, later, and you never saw such a hole. Really—over a mile across on the rim, and you look right down into the throat of it."

"Ach. Just a stump!" He seemed lost in memory of the once-beautiful mountain. "Nature all lavish, building, pulling down, creating, destroying. Chasing every material particle from form to form, ever changing, ever beautiful. I'm telling ye, laddie—it seems enormous waste. But it is from use to use, beauty to yet higher beauty; and we soon cease to lament waste and death, and rather rejoice in the imperishable, unspendable wealth of the universe, and faithfully watch and wait the reappearance of everything that melts and fades and dies about us." And then he was off again.

He was not just a fast walker, he was the fast walker, and already I was winded. It made talking tricky, but I realized I needed only to listen. When would I get a chance like this again?

His attention was instantly absorbed in our woods. It did seem magic to me—after all that city walking, here we were on so-called Forest Road 12, looking to make a turn onto Forest Road 15, but they were just paths through ferny, salaly, oregon-grapey Oregon forest ...

"An underworld of ferns and mosses flourishing gloriously beneath all the woods."

That was a little weird, as if he were completing my thoughts. It did seem like another world, yet all around us was a city of almost two million. It made me happy for my town. "So—is this place 'glorious'"? I asked him, with hardly any backspin on the famous Muir word.

"Two million. Mmph." He looked like he might be choking. We walked for a while before his shoulders seemed to relax a little, beneath some cedars. "Well, the forest here is Godful enough."

At Muir's breakneck pace we came most of the way up the slope in hardly over an hour. We crossed a little trail that led off southwards. "Wildwood

Trail," I said. "But we have to keep going on up to the road—UGB is that way."

He never even paused. How could I be surprised, watching him disappear down that trail, footstep unencumbered and eager as if he were not well over a hundred years old. Nothing on earth had ever been able to keep him from rambling the pure, the Godful woods.

◆

Some months later, I was stopped in mid stride along a country highway by a liquid, unearthly sound I had not heard since I was five days deep into the North Cascades. A flutelike, moistly buzzy tone, prolonged and followed by stillness, and then another such tone at a strangely dissonant interval. . . . Cars swooshed by me on Meyers Road south of Oregon City. The thrush, as ever, unseen. And Muir was there listening at my side.

◆

"I'd like to tell Burroughs about this. Here I am suffering in a monstrous city . . . yet this little thrush brings me all the good news I need." He looked around at the houses, farms, traffic. *"My lord. A howling metropolis of dwelling boxes."*

"Oh, Portland's not so bad. I moved here from Los Angeles—I love the trees . . ." Muir grimaced and I instantly remembered how he met his end: not in the woods, from a bear or a great climactic storm, as would have been meet. But in LA. And from the grippe.

He looked around at the mixed farm and forest. *"I suppose it is all good in a food-and-shelter way, but about as far from the forests and gardens of God's wilderness as bran-dolls are from children."*

An aggression of SUVs tore by us. He flinched. *"Have ye not yet learned the eternal unfitness of civilized things? Are ye resigned to these metropolitan evils? I tell you, everyone here is more or less sick; there is not a perfectly sane man in a city like this. There is no daylight in towns. But up there, there . . ."* We had come to a high point that gave a view eastward, towards Mt. Hood. *"The weary public ought to know that there is light there."*

We passed sheep, a Christmas tree farm, a nursery called "Flowerdew," but none of it satisfied the poor man, who looked as if he were choking on poison every time a car or truck motored past us. He kept glancing to our left, hoping for another glimpse of the mountain.

"Never shall I forget my first glorious view of Mt. Hood one evening in July. I was then sauntering with a friend across the new Willamette bridge between

Portland and East Portland for the sake of the river views, which are here very fine in the tranquil summer weather . . ."

"New bridge? Which one?"

"As I recall the buzz was all about its being steel, not iron, quite the newest thing. Portlanders, you know, always so proud of everything. They point to Mt Hood in the same way, as if it were the glory of the country, the mountain of mountains. Well, as I was saying, when I saw it that day in its full glory, I was ready to grant them their pride of ownership. My companion, dear old Keith, began shouting "Oh, look! Look!" . . . and there across the forest, over which the mellow light of the sunset was streaming, stood Mt. Hood in all the glory of the alpenglow, looming immensely, beaming with intelligence, and so impressive that one was overawed as if suddenly brought before some superior being newly arrived from the sky—like one glorious manifestation of divine power, enthusiastic and radiant, glowing with ineffable repose and beauty.

"Oregon bracketed a certain part of my life," he continued. *"Epochs ending, beginning. I stopped here on my way home to get married, while folks were plotting to get me introduced to important folk—Professor Jordan and so on. Entangled . . . I never got on with such people. And soon I was at that ranch, all those years of sordid work while the mountains called in vain . . ."* He trailed off a moment. *"Then we came up here again and it was as if those eight years had never happened. I saw your forests, your beautiful mountain . . . I climbed Rainier without really meaning to . . . I started writing again. . . ."*

"Did you say Jordan? Of Mount Jordan? I had an adventure there."

"Hmm. Nice peak. They're all nice along that divide, looking across at Whitney. Too brushy to get to, though. What adventure?"

I felt bashful immediately. What were my petty exploits compared with this glacier-striding, storm-devouring Titan's? "Oh, just some lightning on the summit. Got tingled through the rocks. A little snow while we waited for it to blow over."

"Ah. Sounds lovely."

(Actually it had scared me half to death, but I decided to let that pass.)

We walked in silence a little while, under a pleasant smattering of roadside pines, the gravel crunching under our shoes. I knew I was losing him—the memory of Mt. Hood was too much and his hatred of cities too strong. Yet his voice seemed to linger, like that of the thrush a disembodied reminder. Even though I looked and looked I could not see which of the roadside trees he had walked between.

"Shuffle, shuffle, crunch, crunch, I hear you all on the sidewalks and sandbeds, hoping in righteousness and heaven, and saying your prayers as best you can. Heaven help you all and give you ice and granite . . ."

◆

Muir reappeared yet a while later, ever so briefly. How could I be surprised? He has haunted me it feels like forever—--since I walked the Sierras and wondered if he had indeed already found every secret place, every inaccessible mountain tarn I made my way to, in those aching lonely days of wandering.

"This is nice though," he muttered, almost apologetically, when I had become lost enough in a thick hillside forest on the West Slope. The winding dirt road had become a track and then a memory lost in salal and fir and osiery dogwood. I was nearing the end of my journey then, trying to trace the bizarre irruptions and jagged whimseys of the UGB as it included, excluded, islanded, wandered, and jitterbugged from Thompson to Cornell to Burnside, enriching and impoverishing landowners at will, saving lovely lost tree-glens, hiding seven-month creeks that tumbled down from faintly heard roadways upslope, harboring histories of fern and sparrow and chickaree, generations of bigleaf maple and red cedar, nations of fungus and moss beyond counting—and revealing in general that the world was bigger, foot by foot and inch by inch, than any map has yet been able to indicate.

"That little Douglas squirrel, now—only a few inches long, so intense he stirs every grove . . . I never tire of this bright spark of life. We little know of the uncontrollable there is in us, unless we are reminded. An evangel is always ready in Nature, plant or wee beastie. Even these clouds here, glorious white, fluffy, they'll give us a plash of rain soon, and the flowerets of this Umbellifera will be bending to it, all glorious . . ."

A truck or SUV rumbled by a half-mile upslope, and Muir's whereabouts immediately became problematical. *"Ach, it's but a little woodlot. Yet it could do, for now."* He was becoming just a voice now, hardly audible. *"Don't forget, laddie—between every two pines there's a doorway to a new life . . ."*

Boots on the Ground in Sherwood Forest

I walked in the forests of Sherwood today in a blue funk, despite the pastoral charm of the place.

Sherwood is a suburb on the south edge of Portland's west side, tucked into forested hills within the coiling meanders of the Tualatin River. The UGB loops around Sherwood like another kind of meander, coming close enough to full-circle that after ten miles tracing the Boundary, I needed only another half-mile to get back to my car.

Like my whole project, in a way: a circular journey. Normally that would please me, an emblem of containment, self-awareness, contentment.

But today my mind travels doubtfully to faraway misdeeds. What am I doing here, puttering in Portland while outrages are perpetrated? Photographs of U.S. soldiers humiliating Iraqi prisoners have been in the news for a week. Unspeakable fundamentalists have responded unspeakably, beheading an American (on video, for bravado—yet their faces and heads were hooded). Meanwhile twenty thousand civilians, at the very least, are dead at our hands. Bland lies and murderous policies rain down on us all. And I am going walkies, street by street, for . . . what? To notice birdies and nice little houses?

What responsibility do I bear, I wonder?

Or what innocence?

I know that strapping on my boots in the early morning, starting out on the first hopeful mile of sidewalk, riverside trail, or country highway, I feel that fresh elation of a new beginning, as if I had been reborn, as if the day had no history and was nothing but endless possibility. I'm committed to that feeling and its underlying truth. Thoreau, my beloved guide for so many decades now, said it, wringing my heart when I read it for the first time: "Rise free from care before the dawn, and seek adventures . . ."

What does it mean, though, with this shadow across it, the dark flicker of this bird of prey? There are bloodier facts to attend to.

Walking in this wartime has started to feel disconnected. Self-involved. Trivial.

◆

What strikes you immediately about Sherwood is its prettiness. The gentle roll of hill gives vistas of village or green bottomland or fir forest encroaching, edging, reminding. The sameness of these middle-class houses lined up on subdivision drives is offset by all this topography. As I thread along Michael and Highpoint streets, the UGB manifests itself in a now-familiar effect—that wall of fir trees just behind back fences. Views and forests give a pleasant feeling, the quilty this-'n'-that of real life—of nature, even. "Landscapes plotted and pieced" just past the end of the street. I've always been happiest on the edges of things. That's how it feels here. That this street is on its first asphalt, these houses still under their first roofs, is somehow forgiven by the setting. Room for new and old, it says. A peaceable kingdom.

This is noticed with dark irony. I am edgy, hawking for trouble. I don't trust peaceable suburbs, not one inch.

A chat with Michele, caught carrying grass clippings across her driveway, tells me the other side I crave to hear. "Do you like living next to the UGB?" I ask—my lame conversation opener. "Of course! But those politicians keep trying to move it. . . ." she shakes her head. She's a lean and active grey-haired mom, probably my mid-fifties age, has a son home from college. "Excuse me if I'm a little cynical about our leaders!" she adds. I've read about Sherwood's battles with the Metro government. Residents fear being swamped in undiluted suburbia and they noisily resist attempts to extend the Boundary. Like almost everyone I've conversed with, they approve it *right where it is.* Their voices were loud and sustained, so the recent round of Boundary-moving has made only minor adjustments here. Sherwood is safe for another five years. Far off to the east, the less-organized community of Damascus (more rural, more poor) has taken the brunt of the expansion instead. "Oh but that's not our only fight," says Michele. "We tried to stop the gas pipeline and failed. It's right over there." Somehow managing to convey cheerfulness, anger, and resignation all at once, she dumps the clippings and points down hill, where I'm headed.

And I continue down Michele's street reassured somehow, knowing that strife is not absent even here.

But I'm also struck by what I begin to think of as the *graininess* of life: its close-up detail. Distracted by it, perhaps. Two little girls of maybe three and five run up to deposit something in the curbside mailbox, then scamper ahead of me, back toward their house. The bigger girl is skipping, la la la, and little sister is running behind, attempting to imitate the puzzling skippy-step. She trots, bounces, *nope*, tries a two-legged hop, *nope still not it*, races to catch up. . . . Yesterday's play is colored chalk underfoot. Overhead the sky blue is warm and serene, the plantings all around are well-grown-in, the next hill over is forested, a scent of something sweet floats on a current of warm air. Of course there are birdies.

The girls find their doorstep and are home.

Life is lived in these ten- and twenty-foot segments, isn't it? Five minutes at a time. Our block, our house, our mom. My day, my moment. Here and now. The fine-grained texture. "Far away" is a thought, a headline. It's not here. It's not the step we're trying to master, the thing that is before us to do next. Gracefully if possible. With love, if possible. Walk, skip, cut the grass, write.

Faraway battles seem further away. Oh but I am watching this mood carefully, from a short, deadly distance. Suburbanization of the mind? Or just plain good sense?

◆

Two steep downhill blocks (which my knees don't like), two turns, and suddenly I am in rural Oregon. View lots and sidewalks disappear, and I am traveling down Brookman Road on asphalt shoulders under heavy Northwest forest with full green-fern understory. I pass isolated houses, collapsing tin-roofed sheds, abandoned barns. There must be different stories down here, though suburban prosperity is just blocks away. Down here there's evidence of some time having passed, some life having been endured, enjoyed. Here it's obvious that we *do* see as far only as the next turn—the last catastrophe, the next break. Families are holding on, down here. The old truth: Close, immediate, real. Concentrate on the breath. *Here.*

But on this day, my Zen moralizing cannot quite mask the presence of trouble. Bumper-sticker patriotism reminds me that soldiers from this working-class neighborhood, sons and daughters, husbands and wives, are fighting that distant war, somewhere the rest of us experience only in headlines. The next hoped-for-thing is that someone will come home safely. Many more of these folks, poorer by several notches than the hilltop suburbanites, will have enlisted in the armed forces. They are doing the fighting, bleeding, dying. And killing. They need the money, they need the job, they need the chance at college tuition. That war is close by, after all.

There's the paradox we can't solve. We're bound to get it wrong either way: obsess over politics, and it steals your real life. Stay merely quiescent and private, and you ignore what we must never ignore, things done in our name, things done to us and by us, by a government we purport to control. What's real, the near or the far? What's responsible mean? To whom, for what?

Breathe, I tell myself. I've stopped walking. Down the road I see heavy machinery tearing up the far side, just over the Boundary. They're installing that unwanted natural-gas pipeline. Along the road on small, sometimes unpainted houses, weathered "NO PIPELINE" signs show who lost this battle.

I'm left with a confused sense of general struggle, the muddle of here and there, green forest and class warfare, youngsters sent to bomb foreigners while their homeplace is abused for industrial gain. The pipeline was opposed by the people who live here, yet it was unstoppable. It will carry natural gas southeast from coastal-mountain Mist to Willamette-Valley Molalla, grazing the edge of greater Portland as it goes, introducing (one supposes) some kind of efficiency for the consuming public and (certainly) some kind of profit for someone. Life right here will go on, in the form of these charming apple and pear orchards along the rural side of Brookman, with a soon-invisible stream of explosive gas running underneath.

Chances are, the pipeline will accomplish what those suburban activists wanted after all, freezing the Boundary along a line of hazard that will probably not be crossed. Too risky for new suburbs.

◆

The September 11 attacks had already occurred when I started my UGB project. So had the American response of uprooting the Taliban from Afghanistan, which seemed like a good idea then and still does. But the arrogant adventurism of Iraq had not yet (publicly) begun, nor could I have imagined it . . . except that I'm old enough to remember how Viet Nam was started by a lie; how it was pursued for a vague and unattainable goal; how it ended in a slaughter of innocents (theirs) and innocence (ours). In that perspective what has happened in Iraq is almost predictable. Almost.

Meanwhile I'm walking, pretty literally, in the Sherwood Forest . . . where Robin Hood shows up on an Elks Club billboard, when I turn onto the busy highway. Robin Hood! He, perhaps, would deliver me from these concerns. A wronged innocent, he could shoot arrows with impunity into anyone who opposed him. And he doubled his innocence by giving the proceeds to the poor. Everything is clear to the innocent.

It's not such a remote connection. Of the several rationales our president advanced to justify the Iraq war, the only one that survived the first year was the *doing-good* one. "Weapons of Mass Destruction" of course were never found; the "imminent threat" evaporated; no plausible connection existed between Saddam Hussein and the 9/11 attacks. That left a generalized mission to overthrow badness and implant goodness. *Our* goodness: American power, used to install upon the Iraqis an American definition of democracy. For their own good. International Robin Hood.

One thing I know clearly from my work as a nature writer is that America believes in its own innocence. We live on the continent that Europeans called the New World, as if it had no history, as if it were an untouched Eden. The fifty million people who were already living in this hemisphere in 1492 were somehow overlooked. Anyhow, most of their descendants were dead within a century or two. Now our national parks enshrine the imposed vision of a stupendous, empty land, into which we have poured an empire of youthful virtue. A new land, virgin, as innocent as Robin Hood: that's America.

Perpetual innocence is the national self-image that dominates American politics and empowers the Right. Our goodness is unassailable, our motives benevolent. When "old Europe" was publicly scorned by our war leaders, the meaning lay exactly here: that we are new and unsullied. We are America the Innocent. If we act, even with violence, we are entirely just in our innocence.

When President George W. Bush was asked to account for the hatred of those who committed the 9/11 attacks, his answer was simplicity itself. Anyone who attacks us must simply *not know how good we are.* American goodness is unquestionable and unalloyed. The other half of the President's explanation? That they, these foreign warriors, themselves are "evil."

In the power-politics of innocence, the eternal boy-nation is untroubled by any distressing consciousness of its own capacity for evil. It pretends that we (alone among humans) are not likely to commit cruelties when our power is unchecked, not likely to rationalize self-interest by fine-sounding phrases. It forgets all our national wrongs, preferring a Disney tale of clean, clear-eyed pioneers building a nation by hard work, rather than the tragic, mixed tale of an empire built, yes, by virtue and hard work, but also by murdering the inhabitants, stealing their land, driving off other claimants by force, and settling, in remarkable measure, upon a cushion of real or virtual slave labor extracted from millions of people with black, brown, yellow, and white skin.

This un-innocent tale is the one we cannot quite remember. It keeps slipping from the national awareness. In its place is that fresh American Adam, with an ax in one hand and a Bible in the other and nothing— nothing at all—on his conscience.

America is a state of mind that endures by *not-knowing* whatever it doesn't want to know: a forced and artificial Innocence. Such a boy-nation is of course shocked to find wrongs done to it. A wrong done to an Innocent calls for fiery retribution, for action without hesitation or doubt—without leniency, compassion, restraint, or any other mitigating human virtue.

Thus the ultimate product of this assumed Innocence is shamelessness. No American misdeed, no matter how awful, can be recognized. Not even the My Lai massacres of Viet Nam, which the entrenched Right, then and now, cannot admit. Not even the torturing of prisoners, by Americans, in Saddam Hussein's own torture-prison. The wronged Innocent—in the form of an Oklahoma senator or a pill-addicted radio host—looks into the camera, leans into the microphone, and, spotless in his outrage, declares there is nothing, nothing, nothing at all to regret.

Without shame or the capacity for shame, Innocence turns, with deadly irony, into its opposite.

◆

Thoreau lived in dark times of his own, and had to find his own way between shamelessness and outrage, quietism and righteous action. His years at Walden Pond (1845-46) were times of terrible human suffering and patriotic gore: the naked aggression of the Mexican War, the brutality of southern slavery. Yet Thoreau resisted the demands of his Boston abolitionist and activist friends to join the political battle. He said *only he knew* what his proper work was . . . and holed up in the woods to think and write, to walk and while away the days. "I came into this world, not chiefly to make this a good place to live in, but to live in it, be it good or bad." If anyone ever claimed innocence, it was he.

Yet in the midst of this contemplative retreat, one night in 1846, he ventured forth into political resistance and found the basis for *Civil Disobedience* inside the Concord jail, where he was imprisoned for refusing to pay tax to a slave-supporting government that was in the process of invading Mexico on trumped-up pretexts. "Under a government which imprisons any unjustly, the true place for a just man is also a prison," he famously said. This essay echoed far. Gandhi and M. L. King both loved it and built their work on its foundation. Literally millions were mobilized, inspired, and liberated.

Somehow, Thoreau found right action in the heart of withdrawal from action. This is a mystery, a koan, a divine irony—a union of opposites deeper than contemplation or reason can explain.

◆

Caught in my private life, my quiet luxuries of time and body and place. My boots on the ground in the Sherwood Forest, walking in a land of plenty, surrounded by the planet's most fortunate people. Caught in self-doubt and politics and war. American boots-on-the-ground (catch-phrase of the moment) in Iraq, kicking, pursuing, fleeing, laying low. Boots sweltering the feet of soldiers longing for home … or being unlaced, alas, from corpses in field morgues.

What is the point of walking in war time? Or of picnicking, or reading something beautiful, or goofing off, or harassing the politicians into doing the right thing? Strife there, strife here, peace everywhere in the gaps and hedgerows and stolen moments and lucky decades.

I can't say which is the realer reality. I appear to be living in both.

DAVID BRAGDON became the Metro Council's first regionally elected president on January 6, 2003, having served on the council since 1999. Bragdon developed expertise in transportation issues as a private-sector executive at Nike, Lasco Shipping, and Evergreen Airlines. He worked for five years as the Port of Portland's marketing manager, and drove taxi cabs part-time during his first year on Metro.

In his first year as president, Bragdon implemented reforms that realized significant annual cost savings in the Metro Council Office and created the first strategic program performance budget for the Metro Council.

In addition to funding a new initiative to open four new regional parks within a decade, Bragdon established a Greenspaces Policy Advisory Committee and charged it with establishing a regional system of parks and natural areas. Bragdon says he "supports practical and effective environmental action and advocates habitat protection programs that balance the concerns of local businesses, landowners and environmental groups."

His ultimate goal is "to establish the region as one of the most economically competitive, environmentally sound, and socially dynamic regions of the world."

Bragdon grew up in Portland, where he graduated from Catlin Gabel High School. He earned a degree in government from Harvard University. He lives in Southeast Portland and his interests include hiking and volunteering in our regional parks, attending local arts performances, and traveling by train.

David Bragdon rendezvoused with me on the far eastern edge of the metropolitan region—almost to the Sandy River, on Orient Road, where the newest expansion of the UGB had recently diverged from the old boundary and redefined vast tracts of Damascus and Boring as urban. We enjoyed a temperate August day with a few splashes of rain, walking six or seven miles on the shoulders of two-lanes, four-lanes, and quiet country residential streets, ending on the surprising green treat of the Springwater Corridor Trail, a railroad converted for hiking and biking that loops around the southeast metro area and connects to riverside paths along the Willamette. We saw mostly countrified territory, newly corraled into the UGB and as yet undeveloped. It seemed very far from the big city.

Inside Out

David Bragdon

I'm going to turn the premise of this book inside out.

See, in my opinion, the real value of the UGB cannot be viewed along David's route. I'd argue that if you really want to see the value of the UGB, you need to go to SE 33rd and Morrison in inner Portland, where new homes and stores enliven what used to be an abandoned building and parking lot. Or go to downtown Lake Oswego, where new restaurants and townhouses cluster along a lakefront park. Or visit Orenco Station, a lively district in Hillsboro. Those are the places where you'll see the most important impact of the UGB: urban vitality.

"But those places aren't on the UGB!" you'll rightly point out. Exactly. But they are the UGB's most important by-product, and would not be what they are without the UGB. As in baseball—where the highest scoring takes place when the ball is farthest away—if you want to see the real action of the UGB, don't look at the UGB itself, look at home plate.

That's my first attempt to turn your reading of those book inside out: while the original and still-prevailing 1970s assumption was that the UGB exists to "protect" rural areas "from" the city—a rhetorical implication that cities are bad things—the more important function for me is that the UGB promotes strong, stable urban life inside its boundaries.

My second observation may be equally heretical by 1970s standards. One of those old assumptions was that the UGB separates nature from the city, as if "nature" were something outside the boundary and "city" is something inside the boundary. In the 21st century, let's discard that distinction and realize that "nature" should be woven into the "city." Parks and riverbanks and streams can and should be part of the urban fabric, near where we live, not just something "out there" toward Mt. Jefferson.

Adopting those two new ways of looking at the UGB ought to also shape our decisions about if, when, and how we expand it, if at all. Thinking about that is part of my job. (Currently, because of state law, I am forced to consider expanding the UGB all too often.) The Metro Council has to use an arduous pseudo-science of forecasting and hierarchies that drives us to make decisions that practically nobody likes.

What if we junked the assumptions that current state law imposes, and replaced them with one common-sense question: when and where does expanding the UGB make the city a better place? Expansions that add to the vitality of the region are positive, while expansions that just suck the life out of our existing core are not. If we're expanding the UGB for some important new economic opportunity and wealth for our citizens and state, I would vote yes. If we're expanding it for more drive-ins and low-quality one-story offices with big parking lots, I could vote no. If we're expanding it to accommodate good places for future generations to live, I could vote yes. Those decisions would probably be more sound than the decisions the council makes based on the procedures we must currently follow.

Let's not pretend it is a science. The book in your hands is really about an icon. And like most icons, Portland's UGB is probably better appreciated as a symbol than it is for its functional values—though the functional value of the UGB is very high indeed. Those of us who sit through hours of procedural testimony about it sometimes forget about both its symbolic power and the value it brings to our region. Walking with David Oates was a good a good way for me to remind myself what the UGB is really about.

KELLY RODGERS and I spent a day at the end of December, as agreed, to explore this UGB project of mine. Kelly was visiting Portland, her former hometown, on a break from the masters degree program in Landscape Architecture at the University of British Columbia in Vancouver. To her program she brings experience as a community organizer and city planner. When I first met her, she was a founding member of Urban Water Works, which organizes community watershed restoration projects. She originally moved to Portland to work as an intern with 1000 Friends of Oregon, the nonprofit organization that is something of a watchdog over Oregon's land-use laws.

◆

We drove to Oregon City, just south of Portland, and ended up spending the day trudging through three to four inches of new snow. Our winter walk forced us single-file onto the shoulders of busy thoroughfares, squeezed between traffic and deep wet slush and ice water to the sides. Not fun. After a few hours the grey weather cleared to a brilliantly sunny day, absolutely blue-blue by mid-afternoon. But the air stayed cold, feeling more like a winter's day in Minnesota. Pretty snow-flocked trees, white-out lawns and fields; later, long icy pieces fell from the overhead lines and made geometric patterns in the snow below.

This was almost a year before Oregon would vote against its land-use system, but a measure of discontent was already quite visible. I had some cold questions to throw at Kelly, treating her as some kind of generic representative of bureaucrats and planners. She was game to answer, though.

Dialogue: The Neglect of "Here"

Kelly Rodgers

David: Now there's something that frosts me.

Kelly: Ha ha.

D: No, not a pun! Look at this ahead of us. Here we've just pulled out to drive to Oregon City for our walk, and Hawthorne Boulevard Bus Number 19 is stopped in our lane blocking traffic. We're sitting here, and three or four cars behind us too, while Granny boards the bus and finds her quarters. The city installed those curb extensions and then, brilliant move, put the bus stops on the extensions, so that the entire lane of traffic is blockaded whenever the bus stops. What in the world is accomplished by this?

K: Well, curb extensions help pedestrians. They are elements that reinforce the emphasis of the human presence on the street. People walking. Like what you and I are about to do. It's a good thing.

D: Yes, of course—no argument. I love a city you can walk in. Even though there *is* a price: one or two lost parking spots for each extension. Those come out of the shop-owner's hide. See that little hardware store? Less parking means less business. And business—oh god, I'm going to sound very Republican here—well, healthy shops 'n' such are pretty much what a neighborhood district *is*. Sometimes it feels like the planners don't recognize that enough.

K: That may be true. However, "people traffic" also supports a healthy neighborhood. For example, in my neighborhood in Vancouver, B.C., loads of shops—produce shops, dollar stores—line the main commercial streets. Most of their customers arrive on foot, either walking from their house nearby or hopping off the bus.

◆

We chatted a while about city buses, parking, and the general question of what makes neighborhoods healthy. Eventually we got to our beginning point, parked the car, and began finding out how much walking we could actually get done today. Our debate continued in due course.

D: But the main point I wanted to make back there was about stopping traffic. It seems elementary to me that moving traffic is what streets are for. And it makes no sense to just arbitrarily introduce obstructions. Before those curb extensions, the bus stopped over to the side and the lane of traffic went zipping past.

K: First, I think we should note that streets comprise the largest amount of public space that a city has; generally about 30 percent of a city's area is dedicated to streets. As William Whyte (a sociologist and observer of public life) said, streets are the lifeblood of a city and are key to urban vitality. I don't see why we need to devote a good portion of our public space to strictly private use of the automobile. Public transit deserves to have a place there.

D: You're telling me if you were driving, you wouldn't feel any *impatience* that this is a totally unnecessary, totally bureaucrat-driven waste of your time? You didn't want that bus out of our way?

K: Yep.

D: Look, I support buses. I vote for transit. I vote for taxes. Always. Happily. But the thought embodied here seems like a false consciousness: a zero-sum game, as if to be pro-transit you must be anti-car. That's just silly. The reality we live in is that people have cars, and roads move the cars and people around. And purposely designing the system to be less efficient is dumb.

K: All this from a few curb extensions.

D. But as a case-in-point. . . . Isn't this the core of all that fabled Republican or Libertarian outrage? That there are these smarty-pantses who think they know better than the rest of us, telling us how to live and how to feel, that we ought to be happy someone has planned to put buses out where they block traffic. But this is a democracy: *we* get the final say. I think high-handed, pushy planning like this—I don't even want to call it "planning," it needs its own name, like "plannerizing," because it's a kind of inflamed bureaucrat mind, planneritis—anyway, plannerizing like this is actually self-defeating. Over-reaching and arrogant, it stokes opposition and in the end undermines what we're trying to do: make a better city.

K: Any good transportation planner will tell you that balance is the key: it's not about buses *over* cars but how all components of the transportation system can coexist more or less equally. And an environment that is organized to be more efficient for the car is usually less comfortable for the pedestrian. Did you know that county transportation regulations in some places indicate that the "pedestrian is the single largest impediment to traffic flow"? Now who's talking zero-sum?

And let me reframe this question: why are we in such a hurry? It often seems that the experience of the local place is compromised by the perceived necessity of getting somewhere else in a hurry. This neglect of "here" in favor of "there"characterizes many American cities; in the 1950s and 1960s, we were so busy building highways in inner-city neighborhoods so we could get out of the city that we utterly destroyed them.

D: That's a good point. I wonder what we have to do to get it across to our fellow Oregonians, those who passed Measure 7 back in 2000, which undid our whole system. We got a reprieve because the courts struck it down, but that was dodging a bullet. All over the West there's that anti-planning movement claiming that planning and zoning are unfair "takings" from private property owners if they disallow anything the owner wants to make money on.

K: I notice those property owners don't volunteer to pay more tax, when their property values *increase* as a result of land-use regulations . . .

D: . . . which they undoubtedly do. I wish there was a way to make that added value more obvious to people. Somehow the huge value that's created by living in an organized, civilized way becomes invisible. People take it for granted.

But my underlying point is that insofar as bad planning—plannerizing—just trounces common sense and ordinary human feeling, it cannot prevail for long. We're defeating ourselves by getting high-handed and high-minded, and forgetting that this all has to *have public support.* "We're right" isn't enough.

K: I'll admit that planners are getting really defensive right now—a lot is at stake. Oregon is one of the few places that has managed to keep sprawl and urban disinvestment from running rampant as it has in other parts of the country. It can be scary for planners to open up to the possibility of change or improvement.

D: I keep thinking the public buy-in is the crucial element, and I don't think Metro Government is paying enough attention. It may sound like I'm just talking about "public relations" here, but—hey, this is a democracy. It's *all* PR! Whatever people think, that's pretty much where we're headed. I keep wondering why the UGB isn't given more visibility.

Instead, the UGB stays mostly a mystery, some kind of voodoo that happens out of sight. Neither landowners nor officials really know how things happen, it seems. That just feeds in to that privatizing mentality, wanting the government out of my way. Forgetting the value it creates.

K: Out of your way? Like a bus?

D: Ouch.

K: What's happening here is a basic denial that we are all in this together, or if you'll pardon the cliché: we all live downstream. I wonder what would happen if people were able to see the region from an aerial perspective, to notice how interconnected it all is.

D: We'd get the picture: All on the same bus, really.

K: Surely you wouldn't end with another bad joke?

By this time our shoes were wet and we had finished about six miles, walking mostly in the street because snow had covered the sidewalks—but it had also banished traffic, at least on the side roads where we chased the Boundary. But when we trudged back to our car along busy Route 213 we were crowded over onto the slushy shoulder; there was not even a sidewalk for us, as if to illustrate the cars-versus-people theme. Shouting to make conversation and keeping a lookout when we edged along the guard rails, we were glad to call it a day.

Seemingly Paul Shepard

Born in 1925, Paul Shepard grew up hunting and fishing in the Missouri woods, and "always thought of [himself] as a naturalist." His 1967 *Man in the Landscape*, derived from his doctoral dissertation in ecology at Yale, announced a synthetic and wide-ranging intellect, connecting disciplines of ecology and anthropology with questions of human identity often reserved for the humanities. His 1969 collection (edited with Daniel McKinley), *The Subversive Science: Essays toward an Ecology of Man,* helped propel an academic and cultural awakening. Books such as *The Tender Carnivore and the Sacred Game* (1973) and *Nature and Madness* (1982) made him one of the environmental movement's leading thinkers.

He died in 1996 after serving more than twenty years as Avery Professor of Natural Philosophy and Human Ecology at Claremont College, Claremont Graduate University, and Pitzer College. His posthumous *Coming Home to the Pleistocene*—an accessible weaving together of his lifework's main threads—was edited by his wife, Florence R. Shepard, who was an important partner in Paul's intellectual journey. Paul Shepard offered friendly assistance and intellectual inspiration to several generations of ecologists, students, and environmental writers, including myself.

Somewhere in Beaverton I found myself walking with, seemingly, Paul Shepard.

◆

DO: "But I've only met you once. And you're dead now, anyway."

PS:*"Well, I'm like a little coral animal, got my tentacles out there waving around, whatever seems interesting I just grab onto. This is interesting."*

"What? Portland?"

"No. Portland is not interesting. Portland is another disaster in the making. It just isn't obvious yet because it's all new and shiny. No, what's interesting is your being out here sniffing around. Just walking. Looking. Ready to see something."

"Why is that interesting?"

"It's a quality of attention, a hunter's state of mind. Not riveted on one point, but on all points. You've got that whole horizon around you . . ."

Suddenly (as the bad novels say) shots rang out. This part I remember very clearly—it was no ghost or seeming.. We were on SW 234th near the St. Mary's property, almost to the end of a down-and-back which I . . . we . . . were making to catch the UGB as it went east-west over hill and dale. Shepard pointed, whispering: *"Those two guys there, behind that crappy house."*

I saw them sitting on lawn chairs in a weedy yard, rifles resting straight-up on their thighs. I couldn't see what they were looking at. "Shooting up that old house trailer?"

"No, too close. I think they're aiming over by the abandoned pickup. Yes, see the beer cans on that limb?"

They started pumping out more shots—they still had not noticed us out on the roadway—and I walked us away quickly. Shepard glanced at me out the side of his eye with a laughing crinkle I did not entirely appreciate.

"God, you're such a city boy."

"Well, yeah. Straight guys shootin' up the neighborhood, I'm out here alone . . . semi-alone, or maybe talking to myself . . ."

"Listen, pardner, those ol' boys may be closer to something real than you think. You can bet they go out hunting at least once a year, fishing a dozen times over the summer. They know something their Beaverton BMW-driving neighbors don't have a clue about."

I waited.

"When you bring home an animal you spent all day waiting for . . . waiting, you know. Going someplace, quietly, and waiting, quietly . . . when you clean that and eat it, sharing it with your kids or neighbors or whoever, you understand more than just 'where food comes from.' Though that alone would be a big step forward for some of these suburban folks here—the idea of normal killing. Killing as part of living. But more than that . . ."

I thought I knew where this was going. "The Bambi thing?"

"Much more than that. They know that they are connected to the living world, but not in the nature-writing way. Not merged with it sentimentally. They know we are surrounded by a multitude of conscious, powerful beings, incarnate as natural forms. They know there's a dance, an infinitely intricate negotiation, we must do with that world. Our ability to attend to animals with such intensity—this is a way of attending to our own animal mind. Our own creatures, within.

"And when they know that, they know something about inside and outside. They know that this other world—"the other," as academics say—

cannot become part of the self but must remain the alien aspect, a part of our individual being that is not entirely assimilable. And yet they're not separate—separation is an illusion of superiority and independence fostered by civilization. A hunter ought to be our agent of awareness, because he or she is not only an observer but a participant and receiver."

"Those rednecks there? They know this?"

"Yes."

"And these other Portlanders all around here don't? What about this project we're walking on—the UGB? Doesn't that show some kind of awareness of, what, the self and not-self? I mean, the whole idea is to control sprawl, to put a border around the city, find a limit, and preserve agricultural space all around."

"We've bought in to a phony dichotomy of places. We have placed rural and urban life in opposition when, in fact, the two are one, part of the same dream of a subjugated natural world transcended by the human spirit."

"So saving agricultural, rural space—that's not good thing?"

"The opposite of wild is not civilized but domesticated. If there is a single complex of events responsible for the deterioration of human health and ecology, agricultural civilization is it. The best in ourselves is our wildness, nourished by the wild world. People in hunter societies show a suite of characteristics—humility, generosity, nuance, a sense of sharing the gift—which peasants ground down by labor, fearful of shortages and disasters, wholly lack. To be in a community with crops is to feel like a crop."

"Okay, I get that you're no fan of agriculture. But building a city that works—Portland's motto—that's not a worthy endeavor either?"

"Look, the real question for you—for all you environmentalists—is this: Can you give up the city?"

My eyebrows went up. Way up.

"All this finding-wildness-in-town business, virtual wildness—come on. A scholar I like says that conservationists are actually doing harm by trying to convert the lay mind to the view that human artifactual reality is part of nature. What we really need is the Paleolithic ideal, a country of abundant wildlife, rich and fruitful native vegetation, pure water, and fresh air. Otherwise we will remain what we have been for ten thousands of years: a sort of perpetual exotic, never ceasing to invade, disrupt, and degrade the pre-existing landscapes."

"Sort of like weeds? Opportunistic and over-abundant?"

"Exactly. Our human ecology is really the opposite: that of a rare species of mammal in a social, omnivorous niche. Our demography is one of a slow-

breeding, large, intelligent primate. To shatter our population structure, to become abundant in the way of rodents, not only destroys our ecological relations with the rest of nature, it sets the stage for our mass insanity."

His face looked like I remembered, sun-browned and lined but taut, thoughtful. Just a tad dangerous.

"The long view is that we don't need cities. The social, ecological, and ideological characteristics natural to our humanity are to be found in the lives of foragers. They are our human nature because they characterized the human way of life during our evolution."

"So you don't mind saying there is a 'human nature'? That's a big no-no right now. The tide of philosophical and cultural analysis—postmodern, poststructuralist, French—says that there is no such thing. No essences; only constructs. Both we ourselves, and what we call 'nature': constructs."

"Of course the ways we do things and think about things are conditioned, even constructed, by culture and personal history. That's not hard to grant. But the notion that we and our perceptions are blank slates on which culture does whatever it wants is just silly. Our brains and bodies didn't fall out of the sky—they evolved on planet Earth. We are Pleistocene hominids keyed with infinite exactitude to small-group, omnivorous life in forest/plains edges of the wilderness. Two million years of hominid experience have shaped us very precisely. Our brain-body units are adapted to certain conditions: they expect to encounter certain kinds of things—that's what they're for. Obviously a light-gathering eye "expects" to function in an environment where there's light. That's part of the human habitat, and thus part of our "nature." And neither the light nor the eye nor the brain's readiness and you might say eagerness to interpret this light is "constructed" or arbitrary or negotiable. It's just there.

"The same thing goes for us right up and down the scale of physical, social, emotional life. Our bodies and minds expect certain optimum or "normal" conditions. And they're quite happy, quite functional, fulfilled, and at ease, when they find them. And they're unhappy when they don't."

"And cities don't provide these conditions of fulfillment?"

"Only quite poorly. For most of our species life we've thrived in groups of maybe ten to fifteen adults, plus their accumulated young and old, making twenty-four to thirty on average. The most people we need to be around, beyond this tribal grouping, would be clans—a loose association of tribes—with maybe occasional larger get-togethers for finding mates, mixing up the bloodline, trading good ideas.

"But standing cities in the tens of thousands are a complete distortion of the human need. They foster materialism, ownership, hoarding. They

necessitate authoritarian structures of governance, and create an exaggerated individualism as a reaction. Neither is normal or healthy. They lump children together in same-age masses, where the children themselves are allowed to create their own, distorted systems of values and references. In a healthy setup, children are always embedded in a mixture of humans from infant to aged. In this matrix, they are socialized as humans, not alienated as some group ("adolescent" or whatever). It's just nuts to hand over so much power to the children. That's our job as adults: to be the social environment in which they grow up. Not just to speak it, but to be it, day in and day out."

"So city life can't nourish us? Not even in Portland, with a (relatively) limited population, Mt. Hood visible, and forests not too far away . . .?"

"Obviously we cannot simply re-create the hunter-gatherer cultures of the past. What we can do is borrow creatively from them, knowingly. What we can do is single out those many things, large and small, that characterized the social and cultural life of our ancestors—the terms under which our genome itself was shaped—and incorporate them as best we can by creating a modern life around them. Elements in those cultures can be recovered or re-created because they fit us. They are our human nature."

"But couldn't you see Portland's experiment—defining the edge, setting up a strong contrast with rural not-city all around, building neighborhoods—as a step toward the fantasy you spun in *The Tender Carnivore*? That vision of modern, even technological human communities sort of islanded, with wilderness all around where people would go to reconnect, reanimate, what, renegotiate with the living world? Haven't we taken just a step, maybe, in that direction?"

He shrugged, considering. Then—the last word I got from him, faint and unconvinced, as he walked out of my view:

"Maybe."

City Limits

At precisely 12:04 on a Portland summer's day in June, I turned the corner of the farthest western point of the UGB. I stood for a moment looking down through leafy canopy into the greenish waters of Dairy Creek, which carve the curvy limits of Hillsboro. Then I turned, jogged across the Tualatin Valley Highway, and began the return bend of my circumambulation of this town. Now my eyes looked up at the backs of the West Hills instead of peering towards the Coast Range. Now the Willamette and the Columbia awaited me.

To celebrate, I spent some time with the dead. I was hungry for lunch, the day was growing hot by local standards (meaning, O happy climate, creeping into the low 80s!), and an old cemetery offered itself, wedged with no sign or ceremony between highway and creek. First I looked around at weathered gravestones and family monuments. On some of them I read names of streets I had just been walking or planning to walk—Bailey, Shute—implying local families with histories I did not know. Eventually I sat myself down in oak shade next to poor little Edwin T. Tongue (1870-1870) for a sandwich, an apple, and fifteen minutes of rest.

Fifteen minutes is all I usually permit myself. This is a dumb habit, rooted in some obscure blend of ambition and neurosis.

But lounging in a graveyard does slow you down. It produces thoughts that previous eras considered morally instructive: life's brevity, the insignificance of worries and struggles (i.e., ambitions and neuroses). *Our* era considers such thoughts . . . well, it doesn't consider them. We believe in optimism. Our candidates vie with each other in projecting it, no matter what dire mess might be going forward. Our determined optimism was, in fact, on view during the Ronald Reagan obsequies right about then. Weeks had passed since his death but still the flags drooped half-staff, still the eulogies tolled out his fabled optimism. Death had no hold over him! No! It was still Morning in America!

Graveyards, though, do not let you off so easy. I'm pretty sure that's why American churches have abandoned the tradition of churchyards. Their pastors aim to please, now, with a more upbeat, Reaganesque message: *Everything is possible. Nothing to hold you back.*

Anyway, as I resumed walking in my sunny, shady UGB day, I was quite sure the adjacent used-car dealership did not spend time contemplating its mortality. It had SUVs for sale and a squad of youthful underoccupied salesmen—salesboys, really—in too-large long-sleeve shirts. What graveyard? Juxtapositions like this are becoming ordinary to me. When I turned left behind the car-lot and found a more up-to-date cemetery, sporting waterfalls and statuary and, presumably, dead people, all sharing the riverside location with a golfers' driving range, I thought nothing of it. Nothing. Really. Behind tall telephone-poles draped with black netting like some kind of conceptual-art wisecrack about mourning, the range was populated with its dozen fiercely focused males, each staring out at his drive or lining up for it or repeating some inner mantra *backswing slow wait rotate don't look up.* The surrounding cemetery seemed to have no relevance, no possible connection, not even an ironic one. Golfing is an irony-free zone. So is car-sales. So is, apparently, America.

Thinking about death would entail thinking about limits, which America does not believe in. We prefer to Think Positively: the eternal frontier. *Focus on your backswing. Visualize 400 yards.* Repeat as needed.

◆

To trace the UGB along its outside for a while, I dipped down Padgett Road to cross the greenworld creek, hidden in its groove with the invisible Boundary. When I rose up on the rural side I felt like Dorothy in reverse. This *was* Kansas, Toto. Miles of golden wheat, waving summer-tall, and far over the fields a silo and a barn glinting silver. Blue sky forever.

And when the country road came alongside unfenced acres of indescribably aromatic handfuls and mouthfuls of blueberries, those summer rewards for long-rained winters, I thought this one blue-and-gold thought: if half its stated purpose is to limit sprawl and protect agricultural lands, maybe this Boundary thing is working after all.

A surprising achievement, that. Suburbia lay a few paces away, contained, defined, limited. I licked the berry juice from my fingers, wiped sweat from my face with my forearm, thought about the end of the frontier, that migratory flow of the Oregon Trail coming into Eden valleys called

Willamette, Clackamas, Tualatin, and dropping its burden of pioneers like a river depositing a delta.

Surprising, that the sons and daughters of these wandering pioneers, of all the citizens of the USA, should be the ones to confront what the end of limitlessness must mean. Brink of the continent, end of the road, nothing but sunset and ocean before us. And how then should we live?

Stop. Turn around. See where you are. Plant. Build. Dwell.

◆

One of the limits I had been thinking about during lunch was my legs. They hurt. Specifically, the medial meniscus of the right knee, a bit of cartilage whose function is—*was*—to smooth the friction where the legbone sockets up into the knee. Many years of running and backpacking had reduced it to shreds and flaps which the surgeon had removed some months earlier ... leaving my leg just a *wee* bit questionable for longer jaunts, like (say) circumnavigating a medium-sized American city. The other knee had begun hurting too, about the time I pulled out my sandwich.

That was when I started the day's habit of addressing myself to poor little Edwin T. Tongue, whose knees had never had the chance to wear out. I asked: Do you think I'll make it? I meant the rest of the way around Portland. Edwin did not answer me, so I thought of some answers for him.

None of them were optimistic.

◆

The sun blazed (temperately) down. My head sweated under its ball cap. My sun-block stayed faithfully in place on cheekbones, nose, back of neck, forearms, calves. But I felt hot and unclean. By three hours into my day's walk I had polished off my lone quart of water. I had planned to refill it, perhaps from a homeowner doing yardwork. But there was none in sight. Evergreen Boulevard stretched for miles before me, its south side a walled sprawl of tract-housing interspersed with industrial tilt-ups, its north (outside the UGB) just empty fields.

But whatever the UGB is accomplishing on the inside was hard to love. I tried to remember the urban half of its stated goals: density, transit, city textures that overlap to a richness. Perhaps these goals are materializing further in toward the core, where I usually hang out ... but they are hard to remember out here among the semiconductor logos and tracts and whizzing-by cars.

So I kept moving, trying to up my pace to four miles per hour. My usual reaction to stress: Try harder. By mid-afternoon I felt spent, dehydrated, baked, and worrisomely leg-sore. I thought to myself: I'm not even to twelve miles yet! *How* could my leg be hurting already? And *what's* that sore place in my foot? *How* could I be so weak and flimsy? *What's happening to me?*

I remembered being utterly free of these restraints. Once I mounted up with wings like eagles. Once I ran and was not weary.

Little Edwin smiled his subterranean smile.

◆

Americans hate limits. I hate limits. The UGB is a limit. And it is hated, in many quarters.

It works by limiting behaviors: no subdivisions on the outside please; no tenfold profits. And on the inside: all kinds of rules. Like, 50 percent of all residential zoning must require multi-family apartments or condos, to sustain affordable housing. Like, designs, lot sizes, curbs, sidewalks (etc. etc.) must all be approved. We have made a social agreement to forego, constrain, and negotiate many, many actions that might otherwise be profitable and convenient. Forbearance is hard. Obeying inspectors with clipboards is hard.

For in the back of our mind is a vision of pure freedom: America. Hey, it's my property! *Why can't I do as I please and develop the hell out of this?* You can hear it on our local talk-radio any day of the week: regulation as jackbooted tyranny.

The tone is that of angry victimization and resentment, the master-emotions of the right, which sprang forth in the Reagan Revolution. These citizens believe themselves victims of their own democracy. Their twin pillars of indignation: *Gu'mint Is Not The Solution: Gu'mint Is The Problem.* And (therefore): *Get Gu'mint Off Our Backs.*

Of course these visceral feelings express extreme individualism. Only private action is counted productive or wholesome—with an unnoticed exception made for corporations under the slippery term "private." Collective action driven by stockholders and profit motives is, strangely, unexamined. Collective action driven by the common good is held suspect, or worse.

◆

For community is a hard sell in America.

Self-interest has an automatic constituency. Who does not understand a few more bucks in the pocket? A tax cut takes no imagination to see. But seeing the self in the other; sensing ownership in something that belongs to a million others simultaneously; remembering the difficulty of achieving these edifices of intricate mutual agreement—*that* takes imagination. Imagination that builds schools, pays police, supports hospitals, writes laws.

About a year before that warm June day, along a different stretch of the Boundary, I encountered a cop who was selling his house. He invited me in for a glass of water.

Mark Rodriguez was an officer with Oregon State Police, but he had accepted a job with the Tacoma (Washington) Police. He told me he was sorry to leave Oregon: he and his family had lived in this house since 1995. So why the move? He said he'd not been fired or laid off, but with the continuing budget shenanigans in Salem, he felt far too uncertain about his future. "The Tacoma department *wants* me," he said with rueful emphasis—while in Oregon he felt he and the OSP were at "the bottom of the food chain." He did not appear angry or bitter. But he offered me unsparing criticism of the Salem government that cannot bring itself to pay for normal services that citizens need. So he was leaving.

Rodriguez is close to our ideal citizen: a smart, productive family man, anchoring his part of the world with service to community and family values that aren't a political slogan but a home reality. How could we have spiraled so far into the never-land of ideological cant as to just let guys like this go?

We have not yet crystallized the vision that adequately conveys our communal self. Too bad that "city on a hill" is already taken; it's a *city*, a polis, a mighty solidarity, not a collection of surly individuals at dagger-points. John Dewey called it the "Great Community" and said it was, as yet, invisible. Martin Luther King amended that to "the beloved community," locating it deep, down near the heart. That's good, that feels right—for I think it is the *moral* imagination that sees our commonality most clearly. Who is my neighbor? my brother? my child? Every one, said the Teacher. But we must look with the inner eye to see it; we must look past the immediacy of personal convenience, short-term profit, and private resentment.

As I said, it's a hard sell.

◆

When I visit family in California (now moved to the gold-rush foothills), the airport shuttle drives me east through Sacramento's fever-dream of housing—miles of it, spreading over the plains. Every year when I return, the spectacle has crept further toward the Sierras; every year, the driver shakes his or her head, narrating how these hot, flat lands had been rice paddies until . . . suddenly another tract appears ten or twenty miles from the jobs downtown, the freeways fill up, and open space vanishes.

There in the heart of movie-cowboy individualism and government-hating (where Reagan got his political start), a feeble attempt at corralling this runaway sprawl was briefly tried and abandoned. Citizens would not give their own communities enough power to do the job. The result has been an atomized consumerism of individual buyers and corporate profits, the free market presumably guiding all with invisible dexterity. Families in their own houses, unbeholden to anyone (except the bank): isn't this a picture of the *success* of that individualist, capitalist vision?

It is, for those making the profits. Perhaps it even is, for those buying the upper-middle-bracket homes. But it is *not* for the rest of us.

Since the 1930s, Federal policies have subsidized this kind of housing in manifold but hidden ways. FHA loans have gone, as James Howard Kunstler points out, "overwhelmingly" to "single-family detached homes in the suburbs" from the start. After the war, VA loans went the same way. The mortgage deduction, of course, supports it. And what is wrong with that? Douglas Kelbaugh's classic *Repairing the American Metropolis* lays out the facts. Building a house far from town incurs the social expense of providing roads, sewers, utilities for that home. And who pays for it? Taxpayers in general.

Who also subsidize the automobile culture on which suburbia depends. Todd Littman, economist at the Victoria Transport Policy Institute, says Northwest motorists pay only about two-thirds of the total costs of driving (including health, environmental, and public safety expenses). The general public picks up the rest. Alan Thein Durning sums up the hidden subsidies as "massive transfers of wealth—and well-being—from people who drive less to people who drive more," i.e., from relatively poorer city dwellers to wealthier suburbanites. Coleman Young, the twenty-year mayor of Detroit, states flat out that the decline of his city "was planned and encouraged by federal policy." Suburbia is heavily, but silently, subsidized.

Nowadays, as local governments wise up to the costs of sprawl, "impact fees" are charged, but they don't come close to covering the costs. A mid-

1990s study by researchers at Florida State University estimated, Kelbaugh says, that

> the true cost of sewer service alone to a new home ranges from $2,700 to $25,000—far higher . . . than most impact fees, which are also meant to offset road, utility, school costs, etc. This means that new homes, which are usually purchased by more affluent households, are subsidized by poorer households. These studies also suggest that the premium for providing services to three-unit-per-acre sprawl located ten miles out is $48,000 per house, or twice that of a twelve-unit-per-acre development closer in.

Free-market suburbanism is actually bankrolled by hefty communal contributions. The corporate profit-takers are too. But they vote a strong libertarian ticket: *get the gu'mint off our backs*. And why not? For them, it's a damn good deal.

But not for the rest of us. Kelbaugh concludes: "Suburban sprawl is bankrupting local and state governments."

The housing subdivisions I walk by on my sweaty day look much like those in Sacramento, big and new and crowded onto dinky lots, but with this crucial difference: they aren't twenty miles further out. Portland's communitarian solution locates housing as close-in as it can and encourages "infill" on vacant or underused lots. This is why. It is more efficient. And it is more just.

Escaping the in-it-together city for the go-it-alone suburbs is accomplished by silently running up a tab for the rest of us to pay. Leading me to this general principle: *Your "individualism" usually means: someone else is paying the bill.*

◆

Aldo Leopold, the seminal mid-century ecologist, described the limits that create real communities as "ethics" that are a natural phenomenon: "the tendency of interdependent individuals or groups to evolve modes of co-operation."

> The ecologist calls these symbioses. Politics and economics are advanced symbioses in which the original free-for-all competition has been replaced, in part, by co-operative mechanisms with an ethical content.

Leopold implies that if it is "natural" it must be good . . . though neither Leopold nor anyone else can say with any certainty what "natural" might actually mean. It's a large abstraction, onto which anyone may project a desired value. So someone is always free to pipe up: Isn't the "natural" state of an American landowner to simply do as he or she pleases, carving up supposedly empty lands and virgin resources for private gain? Our national habit of thought assumes so.

Biologist Garret Hardin's famous essay about the Tragedy of the Commons put a name to this process. Hardin's insight was that a natural space belonging to no one (or everyone) would inevitably be destroyed by the thousand self-interested actions of individuals. Each little used-up part of the collective would be, in modern jargon, *privatized*. This analysis yields some real insight about, for instance, such "commons" as atmosphere or ocean, used as common dumping-grounds or harvested with no regard for the totality.

But even Hardin fell into the error of assuming that most common space was, in the past, totally unregulated. Research since then has pointed out that wherever people are, they create rules for divvying up access to resources. Most—nearly all—"commons" are regulated.

Consider the people living here in the Northwest before the white pioneers, for instance. They shared this place by means of mind-bogglingly intricate rules of right and use. To take the most vivid example, Richard White's book *The Organic Machine* describes how the Columbia River was intensively mapped by native peoples, right down to individual rocks and fishing-places. No one got to simply stroll up to the river and throw in a line. He'd probably get his head clubbed. Rick Rubin tells of "an almost endless list of rules, different for each location"—"stringent, exacting, and complex." All up and down the river of abundance, families, tribes, clans laid claim to the good spots and passed them along according to custom. These spots had names. They had stories, legends, and myths that reinforced or embodied the rules.

In some significant ways a fisherman or -woman today is probably freer than one of two hundred years ago. Though I'll bet very few think so!

◆

Of course, being "free" to catch fish that no longer exist is an ironic sort of freedom. We have expanded individual liberty but destroyed the living community in which it functions. That irony encapsulates the problem with libertarian anti-government politics. The individual is guaranteed liberty to act but not guaranteed an environment or context (social, commercial, natural) that is not either degraded or monopolized by corporate interests. It is thus only half a freedom: the half you can't use. The half you *can* use belongs to those making the profits.

Call it the fallacy of choice in a vacuum.

At their best, Portland's individually infuriating limits *create* choice by creating a communal context; which, In its turn, generates a richer array of possibilities. No one in Sacramento can choose to live in a town that isn't a sprawling, traffic-choked catastrophe. I've never talked to a single person who likes it the way it is. But Portland's limits have given us neighborhoods, a nice compact downtown, a way of life in which choice doesn't mean: Would you like this tract house, or that one? (Pepsi or Coke?). We have a civic life of reasonable self-awareness, that supports arts and public spaces. And golden fields, blueberry fields, Pinot noir hills all around us.

These are tradeoffs not to be dismissed in the name of a theoretical "freedom" which delivers little real substance. The novelist and essayist John Berger has argued that democracy must never be reduced to meaningless "choice." Democracy implies more: a context of values, within which choice has meaning:

> Democracy was born of the principle of conscience. Not, as the free market would today have us believe, from the principle of choice which—if it is a principle at all—is a relatively trivial one.

It's a surprising declaration for a cultural liberal, whether myself or Berger. It probably leads into consternating difficulties of communal restraints and contests over whose values shall create those restraints. But there it is. The pseudo-value of naked "choice" does not work for anyone who is not a corporate titan. We must choose, instead, to be a community, with all of its hard work of negotiation and yielding and (collectively) gaining.

◆

I miss the springy, tireless wandering of my youth. I do. For weeks and months in the Sierra, I covered twenty miles a day, with a pack, up over passes and down into forests and valleys.

That I'm too gimped up now to get to the end of a city sidewalk is a sad and pathetic pass. Too bad for me. Edwin says so too (though I'm not sure of his sincerity).

Yet I have to admit that the slow, hand-in-hand walks I have been taking with my partner around our mile or two of Portland neighborhood have blessed me more than many a week-long epic in those bygone days. My heart is at peace now. The raging ache of loneliness, the fearsome blistering disapproval of my fundamentalist God that drove me to such solitary feats and wanderings . . . I would not trade my limited present for that disjointed "freedom," not for a moment. Despite the way those days look (on paper) like some kind of nature-writing ideal.

To be human is to be linked by bonds of love and debt, adjusting to other humans who are similarly linked and bound and limited . . . and freed.

Freed. That's the central irony. It is only within limits that real creativity is found. My life as a writer and a teacher of writers tells me this daily. The adolescent has a right to the midnight notebook, full of unorganized blurt and hurt. But what turns it into poetry is the transforming discipline of form, the invigorating encounter with limits.

Our polity and our poetry both work within this gravity.

The way Portland has tried to organize its million-person ménage may be working or not. Elsewhere in this book are discussions of class, housing scarcity, bureaucratic rigidity. But the way to respond to those issues is through embracing our connections, our limits, not imagining a life without them.

HOLLY IBURG was born and raised in the Cedar Hills area of Portland and grew up riding horses and picking berries in the summer. She attended the University of Portland, studied and traveled extensively in Europe, and graduated from Portland State with a degree in Humanities. She became involved in social work and worked for a federal social service affiliate of Job Corps (JACS) in their San Francisco regional office. She then attended Golden Gate University part-time studying accounting and began a free-lance accounting practice.

Marriage prompted a move to southern California where Iburg attended law school and practiced law in the fields of bankruptcy and real estate. She returned to Portland in 1992 to live in her great-grandmother's home. After practicing law for one year, she went into commercial real-estate brokerage and project management. In 2001 Iburg joined Newland Communities, a national real-estate developer with an emphasis on "master-planned communities," to handle community development and public involvement with municipal and political bodies. She says she "deals with complicated and sensitive land-use issues for Newland and enjoys the creation of new communities."

GARY CONKLING is president of Conkling Fiskum and McCormick, a public affairs, strategic communications, and research firm based in Portland, whose clients include Oregon corporations, trade associations, and nonprofit organizations. He has successfully lobbied major legislation to restructure Oregon's electricity market, increase funding for transportation, and protect Oregon's wine industry.

Conkling graduated from Seattle Pacific University. Before directing public affairs for Tectronix, he worked in Washington D.C. as staff director for Oregon congressmen Les AuCoin and Ron Wyden, the latter now the state's senior U.S. senator. Before that Conkling was news editor for *The Daily Astorian* and also worked as a reporter in Port Angeles, Washington.

Along with his passion for baseball, Conkling devotes significant energies to the Portland community. His interest in theater and other performing arts is reflected by his service on the commission that oversees Portland's theaters, convention center, and exposition facility. He is a founding member of the Business-Education Compact, has served on the original board of the nonprofit agency that delivers mental health services to people in the downtown area, and was a member of the board that runs the region's light rail and bus service.

Conkling is an adjunct faculty member at Willamette University's Atkinson Graduate School of Management, where he teaches a course on issues management. He was recently on the program faculty for the "Measure 37 Summit" sponsored by the Oregon Law Institute of Lewis and Clark Law School.

◆

Holly and Gary met up with me one morning at a diner across the Tualatin Valley Highway from "Reed's Crossing," a gigantic tract of undeveloped land usually known as the "St. Mary's parcel," for the local Catholic order which originally owned it. I had just finished walking three sides of it, along suburban housing on two sides, but also along the busiest of commercial streets. The UGB draws a one-mile square to exclude the parcel from development—and I was wondering what the heck was up with it. These were the ideal folks to explain it to me, since Holly represents the current owner (Newland Communities, a national developer) and Gary had worked with the previous would-be developer. We crossed the highway and walked on stubbly acreage toward a huge spreading white oak in the center of the property. I was impressed by the depth of these two business representatives' progressive community values, and their obvious commitment to "smart growth," which they had tried mightily to bring here to this urban-adjacent parcel, wedged between the Portland suburban communities of Hillsboro and Beaverton some ten miles southwest of Downtown. After a few hours, I began to understand their frustration.

Later I discovered more of the story. This one-mile square is prime agricultural land, classified "Class I and "Class II." That's exactly what the statewide land-use system has been focused on preserving. It is the first specific goal in the official list of nineteen planning goals that guides the process (after the generic ones about citizen involvement and planning). The advocacy group 1000 Friends of

Oregon actively opposed including the St. Mary's parcel within the UGB for that reason, also pointing out that the new UGB inclusions in Damascus were *not* primarily high-quality agricultural lands : according to the Clackamas County zoning map, those lands were zoned mostly for 5-acre "rural residential" uses and only about 30 percent for agriculture or timber. 1000 Friends was founded by Tom McCall just before he left the governorship in 1975 to protect and advocate for the uniquely ambitious and progressive land-use system he had helped initiate. And this large southwest-Portland parcel would seem to be just the sort of farmland his system was designed to protect from development.

But agriculturalists I have talked to all around the UGB—farmers, nursery owners, vineyardists—have emphasized to me that farming is virtually never compatible with neighboring residences. Few homeowners will put up with farming's early hours, noise, dust, and spraying of chemicals and pesticides. And the Reed's Crossing/St. Mary's parcel is in fact not being farmed presently. So the question remains—is this urban-surrounded island still a reasonable candidate for agriculture? Or is this an example of an inflexible rule, bureaucratically preventing just the kind of "smart growth" Portland is officially committed to?

◆

Reed's Crossing
Holly Iburg and Gary Conkling

Even from space, photographs show this 463-acre parcel jutting into an area surrounded by industry, a major commercial center, houses, a golf course, and a gigantic statue of a rabbit.

Reed's Crossing sits largely vacant and under-utilized after two decades of being in the political crosshairs of urban expansion and agricultural land protection. Today, the property earns more income from parking for a major golf tournament than it does from its farm lease.

Walking the length of the Portland metropolitan area urban growth boundary can deliver stark contrasts between multi-family housing units on one side of the road and productive, bucolic farm fields on the other. But walking the line along Tualatin Valley Highway past Reed's Crossing property produces something more akin to puzzlement.

Tri-Met buses whiz by every fifteen minutes, reminding the walker this isn't the urban fringe—it is one of the most well-used transit corridors in the entire region. The Westside MAX line runs a mile or so away. A few more miles to the north—a comfortable bike ride—sits the heart of the Silicon Forest, which makes Hillsboro one of the most job-heavy but housing-short communities in the metropolitan area. An Intel campus lies a few blocks away; a Fred Meyer store sells its wares across the street. City officials are busy planning the area just west of Reed's Crossing, which includes a site for a new elementary school.

Newland Communities, owners of Reed's Crossing, want to develop a planned community featuring a range of single-family and multi-family housing, a site large enough for two public schools, a community center, parks, and some neighborhood commercial development. It would be a mixed-use development designed to take advantage of the site's central location close to jobs, the Hillsboro regional center, and public transportation.

Reed's Crossing is intended as a complete community, with houses for families just starting out as well as for mature citizens who want to retire, but stay close to church, medical facilities, family, and friends. Its location would enable a family of moderate income to avoid the expense of a second car by being close to schools, job centers, and public transportation.

Because Reed's Crossing contains high-quality soil types, it hasn't been added to the urban growth boundary. However, land in Damascus, which has similar soil characteristics and active farm operations, was added to the UGB, despite being a long way from existing job centers, such as those in Hillsboro.

Reed's Crossing draws its name from Simeon Reed, who along with his wife Amanda funded the start of Reed College in 1908 and operated a dairy and creamery on the site. He grew grain, but only to feed his dairy herd, which is why he never bothered to provide the site with irrigation. The Reeds raced thoroughbred horses on the side.

The Reed estate was bequeathed to the Sisters of St. Mary's long before anyone dreamed of an urban growth boundary, with the express purpose of using it to derive income for the Sisters' retirement. Later, when the original UGB line was drawn, someone thought he was doing the Sisters a favor by excluding the site because they weren't ready to develop the land. It has been a battle ever since.

The first plans pursued by the Sisters involved industrial use of their land. The Metro Council shot down two separate proposals, one by a single vote.

A decade later, the Sisters formed a partnership with a residential developer that specialized in planned communities. They produced a plan calling for a mixed-use development, with a range of housing options and price points to meet Hillsboro's growing need for more housing. On the power of this idea, the Metro Council included Reed's Crossing (then known as St. Mary's) in its urban reserve. However, court challenges wound up invalidating the entire urban reserve.

Metro then decided to skip setting aside urban reserves and went directly to a process of adding land to the UGB to ensure a twenty-year supply for future housing. Reed's Crossing, which scores extremely high on its ease of urbanization (even without counting its obvious transportation benefits), again was included. Once more, court challenges torpedoed Metro's action.

The most recent UGB decisions by Metro have taken a cautious turn, sticking largely with sites designated as "exception land." This approach led to adding a large amount of land to the UGB in Damascus, which needs a huge investment in infrastructure and roadways to develop, and very little in Hillsboro, where there are jobs, but not enough housing.

The anomaly of Reed's Crossing strikes virtually everyone who sees the site, up close or from the perspective of a space photograph. It grows more difficult by the day to defend excluding the property from the UGB now that it is virtually surrounded by urban uses. If someone tried to farm the land intensively, urban neighbors would complain.

The time appears near when this land, always destined for development, will become one of the best-designed and most attractive neighborhoods in Hillsboro, where children can walk to school, people can bike to work, and seniors can remain close to friends and family.

KATHLEEN DEAN MOORE is best known as the author of award-winning books about cultural and spiritual connections to wet, wild places—*The Pine Island Paradox* (2004), set on a sea-washed island in Alaska; *Holdfast: At Home in the Natural World* (1999), stories from the edge of the sea; and *Riverwalking: Reflections on Moving Water* (1995), written about Oregon rivers. *Riverwalking* won a Pacific Northwest Booksellers Association Book Award and was a finalist for an Oregon Book Award; *Holdfast* was granted the 2000 Sigurd Olson Nature Writing Award. Her essays are widely published and anthologized, appearing in magazines such as *Orion, Discover*, and *Audubon*.

Moore is Distinguished Professor of Philosophy at Oregon State University, where she served two terms as department chair and now directs the Spring Creek Project for Ideas, Nature, and the Written Word. She is the author of a textbook on critical reasoning and an Oxford University Press book about forgiveness: *Pardons: Justice, Mercy, and the Public Interest* was selected by *Choice* magazine as an "Outstanding Academic Book of 1990."

◆

Kathy and Frank joined me on the Sandy River, the first of my attempts to follow the UGB in a kayak. We put in at Dabney State Park, paddled a couple hours, then turned the corner at the Columbia and eventually overshot my intended take-out, making a nine-mile day. Seemed perfect to me, though. Good mileage, good company, good sun. My map-reading skills have always been so-so—an ironic admission for someone on this UGB quest. They were sometimes a problem in the mountains, too, when I worked as a back-country guide. But I always just said: *It's an adventure. You're not supposed to know everything.* On this day, I was glad to have companions who were comfortable letting events unroll themselves before us.

◆

Boundaries

Kathleen Dean Moore

A Piper Cub wobbles across the river on final approach into Troutdale airport. Ospreys soar over our heads, scanning for trout, and swallows zigzag from bank to bank, stitching the water as they snag insects that shine like sequins thrown onto the glare. A man hunches over his fishing pole, waiting for steelhead, waiting for shade to travel across the river, waiting for the rapture to lift him to heaven: who knows. We paddle into the shadow of the I-84 bridge where the air is cool. Trucks thump overhead every three seconds, headed for Idaho or back to town.

The Sandy River is Portland's eastern Urban Growth Boundary. The map shows "urban" on river left, "non-urban" on river right. But from a kayak, both banks are equally sylvan—alders leaning over shaded eddies, sometimes a beach or close-trimmed lawn, a driftboat tied to a cottonwood. I'm not sure where we'll find boundaries on this trip; the Sandy feels more like a seam, where nature and culture are overlapped, folded, and sewn together, creating a profound connection between people and their place.

All morning, we've drifted down the river—three of us in three little boats. We paused above every riffle, lined up our kayaks, then paddled forward and let the current rush us over stones. Wary in this borrowed boat, I carefully follow Frank between rocks. David just bumps down the riffles, telling stories. The sun comes down hard; a down-canyon wind picks up. Alder leaves flip from green to silver. Cottonwood fluff tumbles downstream. By lunchtime, we can see the suddenly open sky that tells us we are almost to the Columbia.

Salami. Crusty bread. Apples. Black-skinned cheddar. David reaches deep in his pack and pulls out three cold beers. Frank and I become instantly fond of this man we have only just met. The picnic is Portland-perfect, spread out on a silvery log perched on a silvery expanse of sand—a magazine layout. No boundaries here between culture and nature, good beer and billowing clouds—it's Portland's premium blend of the best that can be created by humans and gods. In front of us, the river spreads into a broad delta: sand islands, soaring osprey, scruffy willows, all white against this perfect blue sky. I lean against the log and chew salami. But I'm feeling the quickness of the wind, and off to the north, I can see the line of breakers where the Sandy meets the big river.

"Ready for it?"

We pack up the lunch and launch our boats, and before I know it, we round the corner into the swells of the Columbia and the smell of pulp mills. Now I am paying attention to the water, paddling fiercely to keep my bow angled into the rollers. To starboard, a tugboat, the *Lori B*, chugs by. To port, a decaying barge screeches against enormous pilings. Wildflowers grow in the cracks between the decking, a luxurious growth of fireweed and goldenrod. We flinch against waves rebounding from a towering rusted wall. "The industrial sublime," David shouts over the smack of confused seas, the thunder of a DC-10 on final approach into PDX, the screams of osprey defending nests on every wharf piling and electrical tower.

Yellow mountains of sawdust pile on the Georgia Pacific docks. I struggle to keep waves from tangling me in the wires that drape from a derelict dry-dock, also decked in wildflowers and grasses blowing like prairie. The Columbia is Portland's northern growth boundary. But here too, there's no boundary between urban and wild: the city thrusts its I-beams into the river, and the river throws back a damp spray that smells of fish and rust. We paddle miles through leaping water—the wake of the *Lori B*, the Columbia's current, churned by a wing-dam—and finally slide onto the calmer water of a beach-lined bay.

I catch up to Frank and David, and rest my paddle across the gunwales. The Columbia is a beautiful river, a stunner: silvery water and floating islands and green-clad mountain ramparts. Off each wave, the wind lifts spindrift that flashes a rainbow and vanishes. I lift my eyes to a flock of gulls, white in that impossibly blue sky. Mothers and fathers wade knee-deep in the moving river, holding children by the hand. I'm glad to be here, where city and river merge in splash and laughter. There are crows calling, and the sound of outboard motors far away. We paddle on. There is something soothing in the rhythm of a kayak, the one-two beat, the side-to-side slosh, the light in droplets lifted by the paddle blade.

From the beach, a battery of jet skis advances on us, skidding and roaring, spurting in unashamed phallic excess, gouging wakes that slam our kayaks. And then—I hear them rumbling before I see them—a pair of muscle boats. Metallic gold, red. Twin 250-horse Mercury outboards: total performance machines. Dual speakers, woofers and tweeters, mounted on a shiny superstructure, the Beastie Boys thumping the sky. Twin screws raise such a wake that we struggle to stay upright as they sink us in their troughs and spit us out.

You want boundaries? I'll give you boundaries—here, in the way-too-narrow space between my kayak and those vibrating gelcoat hulls. I throw resentment up like a barricade of overturned cars and set it on fire. Nature has no boundaries; it's human beings who create boundaries, building them out of anger and fear. I tuck my chin, dig in my paddle, and dog along through the noise and the wakes, the hot sun and the slamming wind, the smell of gasoline and 50 decibels of *Triple Trouble*.

A mile or so later, David pulls out his map of the Urban Growth Boundary. "I'm not sure quite where we are." He studies the shoreline, a confusion of houseboats and docks. "Doesn't matter," he announces, and puts the map away. All along, he's planned to use his cell phone to call a cab to take the drivers back to the cars. So we paddle over to a long dock and lift our creaking bodies out of the boats. There's a lovely maple tree at the edge of the water, so we carry our boats into its shade and stand beside them, gulping at our water bottles. We're in a parking lot at the base of a road that rises through heat waves up a long, steep hill to an electronic gate that blocks entrance to the highway.

An SUV approaches the drive up the hill. David walks over.

"Think we might rest our kayaks on the back of your rig, get them up the hill?"

The man in the car looks David up and down. Green baseball cap. Red bandana to keep the sun off the back of his neck. Yellow life jacket. Long bandy legs. Wet tennis shoes.

"Don't you know this is a gated community?"

"I guess I do," David mutters to the back of the SUV and the vague smell of exhaust.

We carry the boats up the hill one boat at a time, three people on a boat. Each trip, we wait by the gate for a car to approach and punch in a secret code. Then as the gate swings open to admit the car, we rush through, drop the boat, and race back through again before the gate clanks shut. And it's down the hill for the next boat. And the next.

So now I'm sitting in a pile of boats and gear by a garden between the gate and the highway. I'm waiting for the guys to return with the cars, hoping they get here before the security guards descend. A sprinkler sputters back and forth through the fence, wetting my shoulders. The water smells of river algae and marigolds.

Doublewides in Ecotopia

One clear late-winter day walking down SW Rosemont Road I found myself eyeing one of those country castles people with money like to build. Compiled of fresh red brick, as wide as a poor farm or an elementary school, with crisp white-arched windows and a fanciful entry turret beside hipped rooflines of slate, it nestled into a manicured lawn-and-trees setting anchored at the far end by the inevitable four-car garage. By now, having walked past so many of these mansions, I should no longer be amazed at the amount of wealth this country possesses. It's in good hands, no doubt, kept safe from teachers and mental-health workers and artists and writers—in fact from workers in general. (The world has always been organized this way; I'm making no special anti-American complaint.)

Still. That's a *big* house.

I collected, however, my little tax of ironic enjoyment when I turned to see what was opposite. Across Rosemont in a nice broadleaf forest covering the downslope stood—or squatted—a doublewide trailer deep in many decades of rurality, with an unmatched view of the castle. I wondered how many times the castle-master or -matron must have gazed out the arched window at this neighbor, mulling how to buy off or pry out the housetrailer with its assorted outbuildings, blue-tarped fishing boat, and cordwood.

This picturesque democratic impasse buoyed my steps. I made good time and soon I was closing in on my day's destination: a place just outside the UGB which the map had revealed to me the night before (in a moment of pure kitchen-table joy) as "Ecotopia Lane."

I went bouncing along the too-narrow shoulders of the two-lane, turning left on Stafford Road and making green connections: that surely both those homeplaces I had just seen were, however opposite, some kind of seeking-after-ecotopia. Rural getaway, freed from the galling demands of neighbors, out among the trees and sky and squirrels and weather . . . the American/Arcadian ideal. But what kind of Arcadia you manage to end up in—that's partly luck, mostly pocketbook.

I wondered, though, to what extent these green utopias, rich or poor, might really reflect simple don't tread-on-me individualism. *Every man's home a castle....*

◆

In a kink of the road, some kind of ancient single-room farmhouse loomed in deep shade. Cars whizzed by but a weight of slow time seemed to be pressing down on the heavily mossed roof, breaking it, sagging it over a derelict porch, pulling it out of our busy world. I never get over it, this Northwest death-in-life, the ferns sprouting through leafmold accumulating in crooks and broken places, the intricacies of lichens, the funguses and rots innumerable, the alder sprouts and hopeful hemlocks shooting up wherever they could. This house, this shed—a collapse of hope, a congeries of decay, a nurselog murmuring that everything is just as it has always been.

It marked the street that would connect me to Ecotopia. I turned there . . . and found Jim Kanne (two syllables, he said) working in his yard in old clothes and regarding me with appropriate suspicion, a rough old cob just right for awakening me from this nature-writing dreamstate. "It used to be a small store," he said when I asked. "Fella ran it in that old shack after the war," meaning World War II. "But cars kept taking out the front porch, so I just stopped fixing it."

Kanne had been there since 1959, and he owned some ten lots or parcels all around his place. He groused that Metro had "tried" to include his land inside the UGB, but then had backed off because of sewer and water-supply difficulties. He was glad to be let alone. He thinks it's a disaster that, just up Stafford (inside the Boundary), so many new places are going in.

I asked about Ecotopia Lane. "Don't know *what* it means. Some hippy asked me if he could put in a place down there and a road; I said sure. If I'd a known he was going to name it that I wouldn't have let him!"

That's an Oregon story for sure—culture clash come and gone, and whatever's left just turning green and damp. *Ecotopia* was the name of Ernest Callenbach's celebrated counterculture novel. It rode that new-agey wave that swept uncounted tie-dyed pot-smoking immigrants into Oregon in the late 1960s. The "Hippy Trail" some called it; and for a long while its bearded and granny-dressed pioneers dotted the landscape in varying states of poverty and intentional primitivism. Sometimes I see their children grown to college age, coming into my classrooms with names like Zephyr and Rainbo and a sort of bemused wariness at all things institutional *or* anti-institutional. Callenbach had imagined a breakaway ecological republic along the Pacific Coast, living sustainably in earth-friendly, non-individualistic communes. Nowadays, down there along Ecotopia Lane, the hippies are gone (or grown harder to identify) and a string of ordinary rural homes tucks in between the trees and the dirt lane. Pickups. Camper-tops on blocks. Fishing boats. Same as everywhere else.

Because Arcadian fantasies like the hippy back-to-nature movement—or the manorhouse up the road—are almost always attempts to fantasize a rural life whose reality has already passed by. How many hippy communes sank out of sight into the mire of muddy winters and unrelenting labor? How many rural castles have quietly removed unsightly evidence of actual rural life?

The historical record offers plenty of examples. It's no accident that John Muir's wilderness-worship appeared at the exact moment when the frontier was announced to be "closed." When the old reality is gone, the fantasies begin (usually to avoid dealing with the new reality). British scholar Anna Bermingham tells how the same thing had happened in England a century earlier. When the land-owning class had finished enclosing lands, kicking off the tenant farmers, and just about killing village life, the fad of the "picturesque" suddenly possessed genteel minds, teaching them to appreciate certain kinds of country views—those that left out the poverty and dislocation of the folks who used to live there.

The ahistorical Arcadia: ecotopia built on ignorance of who has lived here or how anyone might, indeed, make a living here. How effectively has the environmental movement reckoned with the lives of people who labor in the country, those who bring timber for our houses and meat and grain for our tables? Answer: not at all. Muir and his followers—and I am certainly one—have seldom noticed them. We're looking somewhere else, looking for that picturesque view, even if it means looking right over the heads of these inconvenient people.

This way of looking is surely class-based. It is college kids and urban professionals who feel put-out when pickups and chainsaws appear in the woods with their Pabst Blue Ribbon, their bad manners and cigarettes and dogs and guns, their fundamentalist bumper-stickers. And then, of course—once they are safely out of earshot—the trailer-trash jokes are brought out by the Goretexed urbanites. Such good fun. No one in the well-educated, well-paid group will notice who is working and who is playing, who has money to burn and who has to burn wood to keep warm.

Because to speak of class is taboo in America.

◆

So when I walked, on another day, in Oregon City on the far southern edge of the metro area, I was (like most Americans) not really prepared to think of class in any productive way. I'm a middle-class kid, blessed with a comfortable life for which I deserve modest credit (I'm hardworking and steady) but which is also a product of gigantic good luck of family and class. Oregon City challenged my class limitations more than once.

True, the houses along the forested ridge overlooking the Willamette seemed nice enough. But when I went slicing down the long incline to get below the ridge—through the "Canemah Historical District"—suddenly streets looked almost third-world: ramshackle houses crammed any which way along raggedy blacktops, cars and pickups parked anywhere, dogs barking fiercely behind fences. This part of Oregon City, crowded between cliff and river, had been an Indian portage around Willamette Falls, and whites used it as early as 1849, so it's among the oldest settlements of the Northwest. Most of the district predates formal lots or planning. Parts of it looked more like Tijuana. I felt out of place and fingered my pepper spray.

And I got to wondering how many of Metro's decisions really address the needs of folks like this. It is true that Metro acknowledges "[t]he magnitude of need for more affordable housing in the region," as I discovered with a little clicking-around research. And Goal 10 of Oregon's official Statewide Planning Goals requires each urban area to "plan for and accommodate needed housing types, such as multifamily and manufactured housing." But I wondered. It felt marginal out there. Easy to forget.

And later, when I enter a older mobile-home tract on the edge of Oregon City, which the Boundary had to include by an odd looping dogleg, I feel it again, that uncomfortable, unacknowledged sense of class difference. It's called "Country Village," and it seems almost like a gated community, with a sales office at the inlet and curving streets. But it's all manufactured homes, singlewide and doublewide, on small lots. *Is this where "trailer trash" lives?* I ask myself (a little ashamed of the question)? No way. Every trailer I see is well maintained and its lot neatly planted. The tiny yards do sport ceramic lawn trolls and painted plywood bunnies and duckies: it's louche and gauche and far from the tasteful landscapes of Portland's vaunted (and expensive) inner neighborhoods, including mine. According to Sally in the sales office where I finally stop at the end of my walk, you can buy a trailer for as little as $19,000, then lease your lot for $475 a month and live cheap. Sally has worked here for fourteen years, seen it all, kept a sweet face and a warm manner. Though I'm sweaty and my clothes and cap are worn, she's friendly to me. She does not mind if I relax on the nice overstuffed company couch while my taxi comes. (That's how you know it's not a *real* gated community.)

◆

So how *is* Metro doing for the not-rich? Metro demonstrates an undoubted commitment to the principle of affordable housing. There's abundant bureaucratic machinery in place for it . . . though whether the Metro/local mechanisms of "compliance" and "reporting" actually produce much seems inconclusive, at least so far. It is certain that, in some large ways, Oregon's system is fairer to taxpayers at the lower end; it does not require them to subsidize suburbs for the affluent. And Metro's emphasis on public transit also serves people who may not own enough cars for every grownup in the family.

But opponents of land-use regulation, showing a touching (if suspicious) concern for the working poor, make the claim that the UGB prices these folks out of the housing market by creating an "artificial shortage of buildable land" that forces people into trailer parks or over the river into the free-for-all of Clark County (Washington), where suburbs sprawl and prices are low. The home-builder/libertarian makes a common-sense case that, of course, if land supply is limited by Metro government policy—i.e., the UGB—then demand *must* push prices up. This is economics 101, basic capitalism.

However, when this assumption is tested by actualities on the ground of Portland, it does not hold up. Comparing Portland housing prices to those of other cities—with and without UGBs—economists find *at most* a very mild upward price effect. In 2000, for instance, Eban Goodstein and Justin Phillips found Portland's housing prices "only about average for Western cities" during the 1990s. Portland's housing prices did shoot up from 1990 to 1994 (when I and a lot of other Californians came north), but most likely the increase resulted from normal market dynamics, not artificial scarcity. Phillips and Goodstein estimated that Oregon's land-use restrictions probably added less than $10,000 to the median home price in year-2000 terms.

You can find economists to argue it the other way, of course. But when I updated this data to the most recent available (first quarter of 2002), I saw two remarkable supporting facts, simple enough for us non-economists to grab hold of. First, that Portland's median housing price was only slightly above the *nationwide* average ($167,000 versus $160,000). And second, that compared to other cities above one-million population *on the West Coast* (surely a more relevant comparison), Portland is a huge housing bargain.

Think of trying to buy a house that year in Seattle ($234,000), San Jose ($451,000), Los Angeles ($240,000), San Diego ($290,000): they make Portland's prices feel like Mayberry's. The two West-Coast cities closest to Portland on the price and affordability list are Sacramento and Riverside. I know them intimately. Both have been singled out for the awfulness of their sprawl. Riverside is two hours southeast of LA, a hot, smog-bound gridlock of unending strip development and tract-housing. Sacramento is the same thing transplanted to the Central Valley. Few would consider them even remotely attractive. But you can buy there for the same price as in cool, green, compact, fabulous Portland.

So much for government regulations artificially running up the price. Portland is the best deal on the West Coast.

◆

Supporters of Portland's approach to planning go further. They claim that the very success of Portland in creating a desirable place to live must in itself cause a rise in prices: people will pay for a premium product. We might call it the "desirability paradox." And Portland's experience in the recent economic recession seems to confirm it. Regardless of Oregon's worst-in-the-nation unemployment rate, prices in Portland held to a steady rise and people continued to move here from out of state (the city's population grew by a healthy 1.7 percent each year from April 2000 to July 2003; Seattle, by comparison, grew at just about 1 percent per year). Portland ranks high, also, in attracting the ever-diminishing supply of educated and energetic twenty-five- to thirty-four-year-olds whom Richard Florida's work has made suddenly trendy symbols of urban and economic dynamism. While two-thirds of the nation's cities experienced a decline in this group over the last decade, Portland attracted them like crazy (a 50 percent gain), mostly to the inner core of the city. Portland is in the top four metropolitan attractors, Sacramento, alas, near the bottom.

And those cheaper sprawling suburbs in Vancouver and surrounding Clark County, Washington—don't they prove the builders' case for free-market bargains out from under the leaden regulatory hand? Hardly. Vancouver's value as a place derives largely from proximity to Portland. According to U.S. Census data, 31 percent of the Clark County workforce goes to work in metro Portland—some fifty-one thousand jobs in 2000.

(Five times as many Clark County residents commute south to work as those going the reverse direction.) Dynamic, growth-bounded Portland is an economic engine, pulling the laissez-faire caboose of Clark County along for its free ride.

Portland's dynamism spills over; Vancouver takes advantage of it. The enormous efforts Portland has made, over thirty years, to attract people and business allow Clark County the somewhat parasitic privilege of living on what falls off the edges. While Vancouver has finally begun to develop some improved planning, Clark County drags its feet and resists even the modest planning mandates of Washington State. Good libertarians, I remind you: *Your individualism simply means someone else is paying the price.* Remove Portland and our hard work at urbanism and there is little market for Clark County housing.

Thus, Portland's housing prices vividly contradict that government-hating capitalist gripe: they are produced not by an unnatural government restriction on supply, but by a heightened demand for the "great place to live" created by that very process of government planning.

Remembering that in Portland, as elsewhere in a democracy, "the government" is *us*, not something done *to* us. Portlanders take extraordinary ownership in urban-planning decisions. It has been quipped that, whereas in Boston folks talk baseball, and in New York, politics, in Portland folks talk urban planning: what's happening in the Pearl or South Waterfront; where's the next tram or trolley going; big stadium project or neighborhood athletic centers . . . ? It's our urban sport.

◆

But do folks living in Country Village feel ownership of this planning system, the way my professional, progressive neighbors or those eager downtown youngsters mostly do? Probably not. My guess is that Country Village responds to a far simpler notion, one rooted further back than America itself: "Every man's home is his castle."

It's a good saying, full of common-law wisdom. Bill of Rights. Personal liberty. All fine: except that the proverb surely also encapsulates the core problem of this book, and of the UGB. A private home is not an island or moated castle, but is nestled into a grid of neighbors near and far which supply it with every amenity by their cooperative and legal integration. The fable of isolated individualism, of an imagined self-sovereignty from lot-line to lot-line, fosters what no human civilization or society has ever known, anywhere.

A strong personal sense of *public* ownership of our town and our system is going to be needed to counterbalance this potent private appeal. And this will be difficult to achieve. Each of us must feel exhilarated at what is accomplished through our combined action. Here in Portland we must celebrate the rising towers and magic spectacle of it all—the public markets and squares, the trails and roads and trolleys, and most of all the festivals, plays, books, artworks, and ensembles that are the music of living, which we can only make together.

And we must be helped to remember how our system preserves green rural Oregon as well. That's our statewide ecotopia—a can-do vision that puts to work John Muir's ecological insight: that everything is connected.

◆

There's no reason Portland's idealistic undertaking can't have support in the trailer-park and pickup crowd, as well as the upscale neighborhoods. Here's one reason I believe so.

On a tree-lined lane that led to that Willamette overlook above Oregon City, I saw an a old fellow walking toward me. He looked a weathered seventy or more and wore a National Rifle Association ballcap. The NRA! I nerved myself to look friendly and start a conversation, though I feared some kind of arch-conservative blast of government-hating.

His name was Louis—pronounced "Looie." He said he walked this road every day, sometimes twice, for the exercise and the view and all. Expecting the worst, I tried my all-purpose question: "So, what do you think of the UGB? It runs just over there, you know . . ." And that's when I got my lesson (how many times do I have to relearn it?) in dropping my genteelly disguised class prejudice.

Without hesitation he supported the UGB and its ideal of community control over development. "I've got kids and grandkids—I want them to be able to enjoy what's left!" He said he didn't want "the city" to grow over everything up and down the Willamette Valley. He told me about a place down near Canby, Oregon, where prime farmland—"The best!"—had been taken over by housing tracts. He just shook his head, saying that land-use-planning obviously wasn't strict enough. He might have been a card-carrying Portland liberal. But he wasn't. He was just someone who saw the logic of the UGB and liked it.

That's our hope.

But Country Village illustrates the problem of people socially classed more or less like Louis, who have not yet caught his larger vision. Later in that year, in the November 2004 election, while Clackamas County as a whole went to Bush, the Country Village precinct actually supported John Kerry. So its voters were far from a conservative block. Yet this same citizenry voted for the anti-UGB measure—discussed at the end of this book—by a remarkable 72 percent, an even more lopsided margin than the rest of the county or the state. These folks, like Louis, are reachable. But they have not yet been reached.

Without Louis's wider vision, "a man's home is his castle" becomes a peculiarly American pathology . . . the American dream metastasized into a resentful myth of personal sovereignty. Portland's success at combining good communal planning with good value for homeowners is simply not generally enough recognized. And in its default, a merely private fantasy is always threatening to take over.

DAVID HASSIN is president of Terrafirma Building. His passion for Portland's inner city and the Pacific Northwest's farmland and wilderness have led him to create a business specializing in green building and urban infill. He declares that "Terrafirma is dedicated to respecting and enhancing the city's architectural legacy, crafting homes and commercial buildings that reflect tradition, while providing modern energy efficiency and convenience." He hikes, bikes, rafts and camps in the area with enthusiasm.

◆

I was nearing the end of my journey when Hassin connected with me. We had a glorious, surprisingly cool and wet late-summer's day below the West Slope near Rock Creek, following the UGB on roads and off, hiking through an idyllic mixed terrain of pasture, homeplace, woodlot, and hedgerow, with a few dense housing tracts in view, and one pioneer cemetery.

Walking the Line

David Hassin

Our walk was in some sense just as I expected—farmland on one side, residential development on the other. The surprising part was learning that it is the richness of the soil that drives the system: Oregon's UGB rules mandate saving good farmland when drawing the line, choosing not-so-fertile lands to mark out for housing or industrial expansion . Walking roads that I have driven (too fast) many a time, eating from apple and pear trees along the way, buying corn from the honor stand along the side of the road, finding the dead beaver in the gutter, reminded me of my childhood in Tennessee: the land's importance—its bounty, and its fragility. I am not an expert on the urban growth boundary, in fact I probably don't understand most of the negative consequences that it has. I do know in my heart that this is the right direction for this city, and in retrospect we will understand what an incredibly livable city we have achieved as a result. Sacrifices? Of course. Worthwhile? Definitely.

I take the responsibility of being a developer/builder seriously. My industry has a huge impact of the world and its inhabitants—manufacturing, transportation, energy use, indoor air quality. I look at my role, even as a developer, as a steward of the earth I love, being part of the mechanism that preserves the architectural integrity of the neighborhoods and contributes to the livability of Portland. I love that my efforts are recognized and appreciated for my company's urban, high-efficiency, low-toxicity homes and am proud of my contribution. I scratch my daughter's name into a sidewalk or driveway of each property I build. So far her name is at twenty-six homes around the Portland metro area. This is my legacy. I am writing my book, the story of my life, through my work—and I need to write the best book possible.

The diversity of people buying my homes is incredible. Young families moving up, older couples down-sizing, single young people making one of my houses their first home, and people who could afford much more. The draw must be life in a vibrant, integrated, ethnically and economically diverse community. The ability to walk to a grocery store, a wine bar, the library, a yoga studio, or to catch light rail or the bus and be downtown in ten minutes. Block parties, potlucks, a neighborhood where they know your name at the café on the corner. One of my favorite summertime activities is the Hollywood Farmers' Market—local, organically grown produce and fruit, fresh picked, has a taste you cannot replicate with all the chemicals and genetic interventions available. There is also something rhythmic about eating what is grown where you live. As well, you can't get more grassroots than handing your money to the individual that planted that seed. I guess you could say my projects are homegrown too, living and building in my own neighborhood. It is the same energy that spoke to my wife and me one afternoon at the waterfront, on our first Portland visit, when we discovered where our journey would end up.

◆

Growing up in Chattanooga, Tennessee, gave me an understanding of rural life. We lived on a half-acre lot with woods and creeks surrounding our property that allowed for hikes to Civil War battlefields without much effort and lots of forts and tree houses. My later adolescence in the heart of Los Angeles was a different world. Bike trips were usually on sidewalks or busy streets for great distances before reaching the large urban parks that served as my back yard.

Adult life in Los Angeles consisted of alternately living in the middle of the city and living on the fringe with horses in my back yard. Eventually the birth of my daughter made my wife and me truly aware of the struggle of life in Los Angeles, and the need for a smaller city to live in. Research into smaller places resulted in a list of about fifteen towns, with explorations to many, and the first actual trip to Portland in 1990. Summertime, walking a vibrant downtown on a weekday evening, and a half day with a realtor looking at properties was all we needed. We went home, put our house on the market, subscribed to the Sunday *Oregonian*, and started making weekend trips to Portland in search of a house and jobs. Not knowing anyone in town and not having a job was a huge leap of faith for us, but there was an energy to Portland that said "Come on, this is the right place for you."

Our first home, a 1930s original farmhouse, was literally one block outside the UGB on Cooper Mountain, a half-acre lot with grandfathered rights allowing us to have a barn, five dogs, two horses, and three cats; it was a little out of place among large new homes, but it was our small piece of Oregon. Work life for me was managing the construction of homes in new subdivisions. We soon came to realize that we had moved to Portland because of the city and that we wanted to participate in it on a more active level. We purchased a home in Irvington and moved into town. And I started Terrafirma Building, constructing homes in Northeast Portland.

◆

As a "green" infill developer, I was surprised to read that the local Home Builders Association did not respond (at first) to David Oates's request for a member to join him on one of his walks of the UGB. I felt it was a great opportunity to experience firsthand what is a sometimes very controversial Portland issue.

I am a member of the local HBA as well as the National Association of Home Builders "Builder 20 Club." We are twenty builders with companies of a similar size, from different parts of the country, that get together twice a year to compare notes. Only two of the members are infill builders (the other one is from Seattle). The rest are building in areas around the country without much regulation, a much easier business to be in. Some understand the negative consequences of unregulated sprawl, some are more interested in their profit margins, but I do think they are seriously interested in urban projects. It is harder to do what I do: land divisions, lot-line adjustments, easements, community design standards. It takes more time and costs more. The easiest place to build is on nice flat farm land, but the price of doing so is the highest: mortgaging the future to profit in the present. And in the long run, for me, this is what it is all about: the future. For my daughter—and perhaps someday for my daughter's daughter—Portland's system of preserving farmland through UGB rules seems worth the extra effort.

Our next Builder 20 Club's summer meeting will be in Portland. Perhaps the group decided on this city for its proximity to Mt. Hood, maybe for the coast, or maybe . . . to get a first-hand look at what I continue to go on about.

How interesting that Portland continues to grow at a time that our economy is struggling. I counted thirteen cranes working downtown the other day; the city is more vibrant than ever. Who are these people? Where did they come from? Latter-day pioneers looking for a better life. In Portland you can live in a glass building over a café or outdoor outfitter and zip to the countryside in twenty minutes; you can live on five acres and be in downtown for a movie and dinner in a reasonable time—you can do all that and more here because of our urban growth boundary.

Whenever I have been away from Portland and fly in to PDX or come across one of our wonderful bridges, I feel proud that this is my town. The people that live here—young, creative, or retired and wise contributors to our city's culture—feel the same energy I felt here in Portland, and come here for the same reasons I did: the love of the land, the rivers, the forests, the mountains, this city, this town, this village, hidden under the clouds, this secret place where it "rains all the time."

Italo Calvino Invisibly

Italo Calvino was born in Cuba in 1923 but grew up in Italy where he lived most of his life. He joined the partisan movement against the German occupation during World War II and won acclaim for the novel derived from that experience, called in English *The Path to the Nest of Spiders* (1947). John Gardner called him "one of the world's best fabulists" in the *New York Times Book Review*. He is best known for the inventiveness and playful, though sometimes labyrinthine, storytelling of books like *Cosmicomics* (1965), *Invisible Cities* (1972), and *If on a Winter's Night a Traveler* (1979). He died in Siena at the age of sixty-one.

◆

From a high roll of the country road, I was pointing out to Italo my beginning point. We could see it a couple of miles over, past farm houses and barns, green fields and woods, and along one side a threatening line of suburbs. Downtown glinted far off. We saw everything, under a sky that promised everything: for this was the day to close the circle, my journey's end meeting its beginning.

◆

IC: *To walk abroad using the imagination . . . this is your own para-utopian activity. But you came back and found all changed, didn't you?*

DO: "The truth is, this part of the UGB has vanished. My starting point is no longer even on it. The boundary line has been moved miles out to the southeast—and my circle is now, what, some kind of spiral."

I drew it on the map with my finger, clockwise, from Happy Valley to Oregon City, over the Willamette, down to Sherwood and out to Hillsboro, then back over the West Hills and along the Columbia to Gresham, turning up the Sandy River . . . then like a nautilus shell, instead of returning to its origin, it breaks free, adding new lands exotically named Damascus and its comical sidekick Boring—new chambers, new cells, added to this growing thing. . . .

"Well, there ought to be a loophole left for incompleteness."

"I had imagined a circle—I wanted to get somewhere and be finished."

"You wanted your walk to be encyclopedic, but it turns out to be an open encyclopedia, never finished, a network that keeps branching. This spiral of yours—it's a kind of model of models, and not the worst one I ever heard of. It's a spiral only you can see. Your journey created it."

"A spiral seems infinite in both directions. The outside end clearly says "and so on as far as you like ..." like an infinite ray. And the inside point, that little inner curlicue, seems to be burrowing somewhere, not just ending."

"Only imagined fortresses, fictions—or building codes!—are complete, finished. The real city turns out to be Escherlike, more like dreaming. Eventually your model becomes a kind of fortress whose thick walls conceal as much as they reveal. Your spiral becomes a labyrinth, the image of a world in which it is easy to lose oneself, to get disoriented. And you are its wanderer. Hero. Picaro."

"Picaresque. Like Quixote: everyone laughs."

"Well, hasn't that been your experience?"

"Yes. I have felt exposed out here, some kind of fool. The only one on foot, rustling my maps, talking to myself...."

"Perfect. The labyrinth is made so that whoever enters it will stray and get lost. But the labyrinth also poses the visitor a challenge: that he reconstruct the plan of it and dissolve its power ... perhaps gain its power for himself. I have always felt the call of the city, far more than my provincial roots. Your UGB is a master fiction, a facsimile of the world and of society. That's its power, what keeps Portlanders excited, believing in their experiment."

"Shouldn't we believe in it?"

"Everything that is useful to the whole business of living together is energy well spent." Italo shrugged.

"But?"

"You don't know your utopia is also something darker. Let us not forget that utopianism was born after the voyage of Columbus. Utopias always exist somewhere between history and fable. And they rise from the same grounds on which city planning was setting itself up as a pilot discipline. Portland illustrates all this—escape from history, optimistic engagement, bureaucratic maze, labyrinth, heroic quest, farce."

"Yep, that sounds right. Portland is a mess and it's also the best thing I know of. There's some kind of faith here that, if we try, we could actually plan something and make it happen. Master it. Get it right."

"But even if the overall design has been minutely planned, what matters is not the enclosure of the work within a harmonious figure, but the centrifugal

force produced by it—a plurality, a guarantee of a truth that is not merely partial. That's what the planners never remember. The surface of things is inexhaustible."

◆

"I keep wondering about that inexhaustibility—do I remember enough? Should I have been more observant? I'm such a lousy nature writer. Where are all the birds? I should have been naming birds. Maybe some more geology. And then, I should be understanding the life I'm walking past. Marx. Dreiser. Mumford. . . ."

"Soon the city fades before your eyes. Like all of Portland's inhabitants, you follow zigzag lines from one street to another . . . all the rest of the city is invisible. Your footsteps follow not what is outside the eyes, but what is within, buried, erased.

"After all," he continued, *"there are many Portlands, each one imaginary and at the same time coming into being. A city of arts. A city of sports. One of garbage trucks. One of sparrows, and one of sparrow-lovers."*

"Which one is this?"

"We walk, so we see the city of walkers."

"And the other Portlands—where are they?"

"All here. The walker's city frees itself from the driver's city, only to be replaced, exchanged—a temporal succession wrapped one within the other, confined, crammed, inextricable. At every second the unhappy city contains a happy city unaware of its own existence, like lovers catching sight of themselves in the mirror."

"What is the Portland of one who walks with invisible Italians?"

"What is the Portland of one who does not merely walk, but who desires to walk around the city?"

◆

His question made me think of walled cities, like those I saw as a child in brightly colored Sunday School pictures—Nebuchadnezzer driving his chariots four-abreast atop the walls of Babylon. Oh the evil, the glamour, the inconceivable distance from my own thrown-together growing-up suburb, that could not even manage to build sidewalks for us to walk to school on! And then I thought of medieval cities, narrow Gothic walls for marching of troops, single-file, armed, ignorant. And then again later, those same walls for strolling tourists. The idleness of the leftover walls, summer sun baking down, tiny European cars beeping and stinking in the roadway, crowding right up to the crumbling bricks, bricks with all the blood washed off them or washed so deeply into their rotting mortars that it is forever indistinguishable, mere corpuscles and molecules sprayed among the grains of sand like scatterings of forgotten stars.

Walls, stars, childhood, everything. It was an everything day. Italo could see I was lost. He took pity and answered his own question.

"The UGB is your frame tale, wanderer. Within it a thousand other tales are told, a thousand other Portlands built.

"The tasteful towers and plazas of the Pearl District, where your journey does not go but which it merely implies, the center you are circling—those are Portland's idyllic dream, a utopia oiled (as these thing always are) by money, as certainly as Florence was, afloat on de Medici money, Vatican money, creating a shining Camelot of civic humanism despite the viciousness of city politics and papal intrigues, blood feuds and murders and plagues, the religious police state of the Inquisition answered in outbreaks of fundamentalists. . . ."

"There's always a Savanarola waiting in the wings."

"Or worse. Cities, like dreams, are made of desires and fears; even if the thread of their discourse is secret, their rules are absurd, their perspectives deceitful, and everything conceals something else. What is Portland concealing?"

We had come up another rise. A moment of sunshine illuminated downtown, Marquam Hill with its hospitals and medical research towers. "Portland seems to want to hold its head up, to be first among cities. Yet at the same time it craves anonymity. We put up a statue, 'Portlandia,' ten times life size . . . but then we hid it behind trees. Even standing right across the street, it's always playing peekaboo. And there we put a poem celebrating 'stillness somewhere deep in the earth.' Is Portland a metropolis or some kind of self-discovery seminar?

"And when we started arranging that aerial tram to go up to the medical school, the official talk was all about creating a 'postcard,' a unique and memorable icon—our Eiffel Tower. But when the decision came, it chose none of the bold, striking plans—no—but a design that seemed to be disappearing: a tram with invisibly slender towers, gondolas to blend with the clouds . . . and a lower terminus hidden under a huge mat of grass!"

"The invisible postcard." Italo smiled; I could see he liked that. *"Perhaps there is no deeper fear than discovery, after all. For then all your illusions are put to the test—the harsh light of day."*

"But it makes me dizzy, sometimes, Portland's simultaneous pursuit of excellence and mediocrity."

"The more enlightened our houses are, the more their walls ooze ghosts. Dreams of progress and reason are haunted by nightmares. That's why your utopia begins to resemble a labyrinth as you walk it. It is full of dead ends, tangles of intent and self-defeat. And most of all the unspoken, that which you remain silent about. What is a language vacuum if not a vestige of taboo, of a ban on mentioning something?

"That's what stories are for: to speak the unspeakable, to find the myth, the hidden part of every story, the buried part, the region that is still unexplored because there are as yet no words to enable us to get there."

We had stopped while for the hundredth time I examined the map. The UGB had taken another incomprehensible turn, a right-angle off the country highway we walked, arbitrarily jogging around one or two acres where a rural nursery lined up its muddy rows of trees and shrubs.

It was mysterious, that jagged swerve on the map. It wanted explaining. Suddenly it seemed we both wanted a story. So I began one.

◆

"Here is an acre owned by a disappointed nurseryman. He alone, among all his neighbors, has been denied the sure thing of urban land speculation.

"He protested but in the next round the main boundary, leaping far beyond this street, forgot to correct the square jog it had left here. The nursery stayed excluded, a leafy island encircled by the UGB, soon crowded on all sides by tract housing. No reason was ever given for the exclusion. He wrote letters, was ignored, tried bribery, threats on radio talk shows, and died an angry Republican.

"The nurseryman's heirs abandoned the property, uninterested in hard work and disappointed of the promised windfall. Fruit trees and ornamental maples left to themselves flourished amid grapes that grew roots through burlap-bundles and dropped annual clusters into ever-denser tufts of phlox and bishopsweed overhung by now with tall unkempt roses and elaborate swaying columbines. Among all the nursery plants a slow Darwinism cut down many but blessed a few, which over the brief century of Portland's ascendancy nativized themselves, fought with blackberries for space, settled in for the millennia to come, more long-sighted than the city planners, who believed their utopia would last forever behind its wall of good intentions and increasingly maze-like bureaucracies."

My voice had risen to a sort of operatic pitch but I continued anyway. The hills rolling greenly in all directions seemed almost vicious in their naivete, a bucolic simplicity studded with three-car garages and three-ton Cadillac

SUVs that seemed to call forth something big, something science-fiction, some epic of disappointment.

"One day many years later, the daughter of the daughter of the son of the nurseryman bought a house in the decaying tract next door: for by then the UGB had grown so far that the tide of gentrification had long since stopped, though rules were still enforced with a religious and incomprehensible zeal. Houses like this went for ever-cheaper prices as their lousy T-111 siding warped up and peeled, rain seeped in and houses filled with people who, generations earlier, would have settled in trailer parks or worse. The great-granddaughter did not know of her connection to the brambly flowery woods next door. It had trails only ten-year-olds could navigate.

"Her ten-year-old did, in fact, find his way there. The mother was depressed, hardly working. When the child brought home flowers for her, fresh grapes, rough-skinned pears, her eyes barely opened in the darkened room. But in the woods there were other children, feral and adventurous, dirty-faced children who parented each other and made a pact: that they would leave.

"And when their voices changed and they began, shyly, to hold hands, they did leave, in brave twos and threes. All over the decaying town, the ones who by luck or blessing still had some green wood in them began to leave. No one moved to Portland any more; no longer did its dream of a saner life lived in a humane and public place draw people from all over. Now the dream was of leaving.

"But brambles and maples and roses did not leave. The T-111 disappeared at last from the face of the earth, and the house of the descendant of the nurseryman became a tumulus, a barrow, a mound of berries and rose blossoms beside a field so abundant of flowers and fruits you might have thought it paradise—or utopia."

◆

I was proud of my story. But Italo pursed his lips. *"No, no. That is not the ending.*

"The mother tells the boy not to go. He will not listen, so she rouses herself, there in the dark disheveled room; for the first time in months she speaks more than a word or two and tells him this legend: that when the woods have taken over again, then and only then will Portland revive. This boy believes it, he does not want to but he cannot help himself: he knows it is true. So he lives out his life silently beside his mother, marrying and making children, looking out at the green spaces gradually connecting with each other, year by year, fulfilling

the prophecy that all would be forest again, so that some descended citizen, looking at the rivers and how they went between mountains to all the world, and thinking of his fellow citizens, how they cooked and gathered and laughed, would begin building again the city of the humane and public dream.

"But this one square of land, beside the house, would never be built on. No one planned this; it is simply what happened. The nurseryman's acre would be green forever, through all the cycles of Portland's dreaming and undoing."

By now our steps had begun to play out the spiral's open end. Ahead of us was the Clackamas River, and beyond it could be seen the new lands that an incomprehensible bureaucracy had declared "urban," despite every indication otherwise. Neither town nor tower, street lamp nor familied street could be seen. Nothing but open space, blotched with ranchettes, and moonrise beaming down the river, so big and round above Mt. Hood that we felt we might be able to touch it. . . .

◆

"Utopia is not a city that can be founded by us but one that can found itself in us, build itself brick by brick in our ability to imagine it, to think it ... Portland, like any real city, is a city that claims to inhabit us, not to be inhabited, makes us possible inhabitants of a third city, different from utopia and different from all the habitable or uninhabitable cities of today."

ERIC D. LEMELSON owns and manages Lemelson Vineyards, a
certified organic producer of pinot noir and other varietals located
near Carlton, Oregon. Born and raised in New Jersey, Lemelson
moved to Oregon in 1979 to attend Reed College. He received
his B.A. in American Studies in 1981. In 1992, he received a J.D. in
environmental and natural resources law from Lewis and Clark Law
School in Portland, and has been a member of the Oregon State Bar
since 1993.

Prior to entering the wine business, he directed a the Northwest
Water Law and Policy Project at Lewis and Clark Law School, worked
as a legal intern in the governor's office as a water policy analyst,
worked in Oregon politics, taught yoga, and played in a rock and
roll band. He is also a trustee of the Lemelson Foundation, a family
foundation that encourages invention and innovation to improve
human lives and promote sustainable development in the United
States and in developing countries in Central America, Africa, and
Asia.

◆

We met at Lemelson's winery in the rolling hills of Yamhill County,
a landscape sometimes compared to that of Tuscany. My walk was
finished. The harvest was in, the damp November day gave an umbery
richness to the patchwork of forest, vineyards, and open fields,
and though we were less than twenty miles outside the Boundary,
Portland felt a world away. But the consequences of the November
elections were all too present. What would happen to places like this,
if planning were abandoned? What would happen to Oregon's rural
economy? The wine industry contributed an astonishing $1.4 billion
to the state's annual economy by 2004. What struck my eye was not
just aesthetics. It was a healthy, productive, varied landscape.

A View from the Vineyard

Eric Lemelson

Many Oregonians, even those in the wine business, don't realize how important land-use planning has been to our success. The proximity to Portland that provided a small but steady stream of local customers to the early wineries turned out to be a double-edged sword, because development pressure threatened to gobble up much of the best vineyard land for hillside subdivisions.

Sensing the threat, Oregon winegrowers and winemakers lobbied the legislature and local governments in the 1970s to protect existing and potential vineyard land in the hills surrounding Portland and throughout the Willamette Valley. They knew that all of the world's great viticultural regions, from France to Italy to the Napa Valley, developed over time with strong protections in place to protect valuable vineyard land from urban and suburban encroachment. They also knew that it would take decades, perhaps even several generations, to discover and plant the best vineyard sites that would make truly world-class wines.

Many of the Northwest's most respected wineries are less than forty minutes by car from downtown Portland. Drive that far from many other major metropolitan areas and you'll still be in suburbs, with farmland beyond the horizon. Yet several of the state's oldest and best-known producers are just a few miles from the Urban Growth Boundary of Beaverton and other suburban towns.

◆

I arrived in Portland on a warm August afternoon in 1979, headed for Reed College in Southeast Portland. Although I had been living in Vermont for two years before moving to Oregon, I was born and raised in suburban New Jersey. Looking back through the lens of childhood memories, calling Jersey the "The Garden State" was an ironic choice. The last open space in our neighborhood went under the bulldozer before my tenth birthday, as old gnarly maple trees, young pines, and a small wetland were sacrificed for another cul-de-sac housing development.

I had heard stories about Oregon's beautiful and varied landscapes, of rain that supposedly never stopped, of enormous mossy evergreens that thrived in the soggy climate, and of salmon runs that still impressed visitors.

I had never actually seen the Pacific Northwest, except in photographs, and didn't know a soul when I arrived. But friends who had been to Oregon told me it was a special place, with friendly people and a reputation for blazing a different path from much of the rest of the country.

I remember that first week, riding a yellow school bus on a field trip with other new students to the coast. As we bounced along on the highway and I chatted with the cute girl sitting across from me, I noticed how quickly city turned to farm, and farm to forest. Sere tans and browns of late-summer fields in the Willamette Valley gave way to the lush dark green of Douglas-firs in the hills, and the stillness of the lower Columbia River beyond leading to the Pacific Ocean's grey-green waves.

Later, on weekends and holidays, I began to explore my surroundings, especially the Valley. I loved the hillsides covered in Douglas-fir and Oregon oak; the orchards; the fertile farmlands that supported an agriculture as diverse as anything I had seen; and the rivers and streams that started in the hills before meandering through the valley bottoms.

Several years later, a friend at Reed wrote his political science thesis about Oregon's land-use planning laws, then in their infancy. Tom McCall was still around, and the system he helped create had already survived several attempts by developers and "property rights" advocates to eliminate it at the ballot box. I was interested in public policy, so I listened carefully to my friend's stories.

To a fugitive from shopping mall and freeway hell, a system that preserved farm and forest land while providing for slow, sane growth of urban areas seemed pretty revolutionary. It also seemed conservative, in the best, Teddy Rooseveltian sense of the word, conserving land and resources wisely, protecting farming and forestry as critical parts of Oregon's economy, and saving open space to assure everyone's quality of life. I learned a lot secondhand from my friend's internship at 1000 Friends of Oregon, the citizens' group that McCall started to protect the nascent land-use system.

Later in the 1980s, I decided to go to law school to study environmental law. The original Earth Day celebration had happened when I was entering adolescence in the early '70s, and had a profound impact on me. I recall vividly a musical my fifth-grade class produced on the environment, which ended with all the kids on stage collapsing to the floor after breathing polluted air. The '70s was also a time when citizen activism really did seem capable of changing the world for the better. I think that this was when the Pacific Northwest began to capture the nation's imagination, perhaps because it symbolized the beginnings of a new relationship between people and the land.

Several years into the process of law school I felt my soul being stifled, so I took a year off to reconnect with the passion that had motivated me in the first place. One summer day during that hiatus, I was reading the local paper and happened upon an ad for a small farm located on a place called Parrett Mountain.

Not knowing where Parrett Mountain was, I called the real estate agent on a whim. A month later, after tromping all over the area, I bought a small farm with an old house located on a beautiful, somewhat isolated, hillside facing glacier-covered Mt. Hood in the distance. I guess I was listening to my intuition, as well as my desire to live outside of the city, learn something about farms and farming, and get my hands dirty. I sold my home in town and moved full-time out to the country. Although I worked for several years directing a water policy research center after finishing law school, I found myself drawn much more strongly to the land, rather than to abstract concepts of natural resource management and regulation.

My farm had an old hazelnut orchard and a weedy field in front of the house. West and south of the house lay acres of forest, with ferns, Douglas-fir, Western red cedar, maples, Pacific yew, and many other species of plants. A canyon with a year-round creek started just behind my back door, and some of the cedar trees in the creek bottom were hundreds of years old.

While it was hardly wilderness, my little paradise was nineteen miles from downtown Portland and perhaps three miles from Sherwood's Urban Growth Boundary. When I arrived at home from my city job, I felt like I was a hundred miles from anywhere. Oregon's land-use laws protected the area's farm and forest land from development, even though it was, in fact, only a few minutes by car from a city of over a million people. And while the town of Sherwood began to grow rapidly a few years later, I knew that its growth would stop at the Boundary and not continue to gobble up every farm between me and that invisible line.

I soon discovered that Oregon wine country started just on the other side of the hill. On weekends I continued my explorations of the Willamette Valley. Soon I was spending more time going to wineries and talking to growers and winemakers than I was visiting friends in Portland. One noted local winemaker told me of my farm's potential for growing winegrapes. At about the same time, I sampled a bottle of '93 Beaux Freres pinot noir at a Portland restaurant. That night, I wondered if I could make a wine that good.

My conversations and discoveries soon planted a seed that began to grow into a serious interest in winegrowing. The next spring, I planted two acres of grapes in the field in front of my house. I spent that summer tending the vineyard on weekends after coming home from my job in the city, and found I loved the work. Once I had a taste of farmwork, I wanted more. By the summer of 1996 I was searching the hills in the heart of wine country for a farm where I could plant a more serious vineyard and build a winery. I was hooked.

Only later would I realize that Oregon's wine business is a relatively new phenomenon. The folks we consider the "pioneers" didn't start planting until the late '60s, and much of the industry's growth happened in the 1990s, when Oregon's ability to produce consistent quality wines began to attract attention outside of the region, and even internationally. Today, Lemelson wines are sold all over the U.S., and we recently started exporting to Europe and Asia; but the first wave of grape growers survived because their wineries were close to Portland, where the bulk of their early customers lived. The UGB made that possible.

I guess I recognized a long time ago that Oregon's land-use planning system represented a new way of thinking about our relationship with the land, one built on a foundation of respect and humility grounded in a strong sense of community. That's what appealed to me on a deep level, because it symbolized much of what is unique and admirable about Oregon.

Contrast this with the perspective that defines the "highest and best use" of land in terms of the present and of short-term, one-time financial gain benefiting individuals, as if they were living in a castle with a moat and a drawbridge and had no connection with their neighbors or their community.

In the wine business, especially, a short-term perspective is the height of foolishness. That's because grapevines can live as long as human beings, and wine quality improves significantly as vines age. As a business owner in a capital-intensive enterprise, I also know that the cost of planting a modern vineyard is often recouped only over several generations. I see long-term farmland protection and wise management of urban growth as both essential to preserving the long-term viability of Oregon's wine business, and I know many other grape growers and winemakers agree with me.

Native Americans made decisions with the interests of seven generations of descendants in their minds. I think we would be wise to incorporate that kind of thinking into our own decision making, if we are to shape a bountiful future for our grandchildren and those that follow.

Epilogue

A Democracy of Water

Six weeks after I finished walking and kayaking Portland's Urban Growth Boundary, a statewide vote overturned the whole thing, apparently.

I knew trouble was coming by the last days of my journey. Polls and airwaves were full of omens. Having seen the city whole, I knew I would now need to see how it fit into these larger contexts—Oregon politics; the nationwide drift toward profit-taking privatism; the contested border between individual property rights and community well-being. I tried to collect my thoughts. Parts and wholes: individuals and communities: inside and outside: mine and not-mine.

◆

On a late-summer's day, second-to-last of my journey, I rested my paddle on the kayak and stared out across the green Columbia, over the quiet pastoral of Hayden Island with its munching, dopey-eyed cows and past the space I knew was occupied by the Columbia's other channel just beyond the island. What arrested me was the strangely pleasing sight of five or six towering derricks, their black girder-tops gliding above the trees and cows and drifting kayakers. It was the Port of Portland's Terminal Six, an impressive industrial structure in a busy paved complex I had visited months earlier. Now I was sliding waterside, following the UGB along its northern edge, from Gresham to Portland and from the Sandy River to the Willamette. My oldest hiking buddy was in the other kayak, it was the tired end of a twenty-mile day, and as we turned to beach ourselves at Kelley Point we watched a cargo ship turn massively in front of us onto the Willamette. A kayaker's eyes are only two feet above the water; it's a critter's view, a river-surface view, lowly in the very best sense. And believe me, from that perspective a derrick or a cargo ship is big. A city is big.

But then, so is a river.

There's a democracy of water which it's hard to overlook when you're on it. The forty miles of Clackamas, Willamette, Sandy, and Columbia I kayaked, the countless creeks and streams I walked beside or crossed on foot: all that flowing together, each drop of it, that might have started as runoff from someone's back yard or as raindrops hitting the summit of Mt Hood. Here they come, democratically confluent. And these waters will flow right through us, too, entering and leaving effortlessly. Such intimate and extravagant coursings, from mountain slope to mouth to membrane—then out again to oceans and clouds and mountains—make a mockery of our definitions of "inside" and "outside." We invest so much of ourselves in hard-shelled definitions of *me*—my skin, my house, my family, my rights—as if their boundaries were not comically porous. The *other*, the not-me, swarms us, joins us, sweeps us along. Continually. Lewis Thomas (in *Lives of a Cell*) jokes that it takes a lot of denial to sustain our pet illusion of separateness.

I like being independent and on some level this is disturbing news. I don't want to be an insect in the hive and I don't want commissars or mullahs telling me what to do. Anti-government talk-show rhetoric exploits this feeling, and does its best to work up anecdotal outrage at jackbooted repression. I'm always amazed at the weird, unhinged anger that results. It's typical of what a half-truth can accomplish: since there *are* a lot of ways we tell each other what to do.

Our society celebrates a manufactured myth of individualism to help us ignore our connectedness. It takes an opened imagination to see the larger, truer vision of what it means to be human—what it means to wear your parents' genes around and pass them along, what the sharing of food and language and ideas really imply: that only together are we fully human. If you want, you can see this as an *expansion* of self: that you are not limited to your meager boundaries; that body, mind, and spirit extend deep into your surround and beyond; that you are more capacious, more detailed, more expansive than you had imagined.

◆

Measure 37 overturned thirty-one years of progressive community planning, citizen input, and technical expertise. All that I saw on my long walk and float—a countryside of wheat and berries and vineyards, a compact and thriving city—has been threatened by a single vote in November 2004.

The language of its ballot title was deceptively appealing: "Governments must pay owners, or forego enforcement, when certain land use restrictions reduce property value." The statute provides that anyone who owned land when a restriction was imposed on it may appeal and be paid for any loss of value (even speculative value), or be exempted from the restriction. The probability is that no local or regional government will have the money to pay such claims, and thus will have to waive the regulations in question. A neighbor who bought later will not have the same right. In fact, if an owner has *inherited* the property, he or she will have rights which no other citizen has, going back as far as the grandparents' generation. Measure 37 was upheld in the state Supreme Court in February 2006, and the state subsequently entered an era of unlimited private claims to undo nearly all community controls on development of urban lands and farmlands alike. The Governor has constituted a three-year "Big Look" committee to recommend a new land-use system that honors communities as well as private owners—meaning that Oregonians will once again have to find their ability to share a vision.

The passage of Measure 37 is, to date, the greatest success of the so-called "takings" movement, which has been brewing in the West since libertarian guru Richard Epstein's 1985 book of the same name. But Measure 37 is merely the second coming of the similar Measure 7, which passed in 2000 but was struck down by the Oregon Supreme Court. In the Voters' Pamphlet for that measure, the Libertarian Party in Oregon voiced this dangerously simple view: "Your property belongs to you. . . .When government officials enact regulations that strip a property of its value," they "trample the rights of innocent people." Emotionally, the metaphor tells all: the citizen shamefully denuded and trampled (there are those jackboots). At the foundation of this outrage is the unexamined assumption—the fantasy—of individual action untrammeled by consideration of any other living being whatever: a condition almost no human has ever lived in, a false god, an adolescent fantasy.

Logically, this argument ignores what the legal scholars call "reciprocity of advantage": the surround of social order and mutuality—schools, police, marketplace, etc.—that is a huge portion of any property's "value," a value thus created by those many other people who have no deed to the land, but whose interests are deeply implicated in it. Ignoring this wider truth, Measure 37 enacts a libertarian fantasy that an owner possesses a near-absolute property right, as if each piece of land were located on a one-person planet.

And this strange notion of sovereignty is not what any sane person really wants, anyway. What we want is to have *enough* control of our lives, while being meaningfully connected to each other: to wife, to husband, to lover, to kids, to neighbors, to community, to political leaders, to the earth, to God. These connections are the interlocking meshes that truly support us, a loving hammock for the heart, each strand a filament of kindness, restraint, forbearance, receptivity, gifting, getting. What community means, in simple reality, is the trusting, painstaking process of creating these bonds and by them expanding and enriching our lives.

But such trust is easily broken.

◆

Measure 37 embodies that privatizing, community-destroying trend that has been dismantling our civic institutions and impoverishing our lives together for some decades now. In my neighborhood are beautifully made two-story schools—Hosford, Abernethy—built in the nineteen-twenties. As I walk by, I often ask myself: Why could *they,* in their time, afford to build these handsome buildings, when *we* can hardly find the money to maintain them? Most towns have public buildings that raise the same questions.

I'm not an economist, I'm just a guy who walks by and wonders. But part of the answer may be visible in these easily available tax facts. In 1943 corporations paid about 40 percent of Federal revenues; but in 2003 they paid just 7.4 percent (while up to 60 percent of corporations are paying nothing at all). Tax rates on the wealthiest citizens have been dropping: capital gains taxed at 35 percent in 1980 are taxed at 15 percent today; George W. Bush has lowered taxes on investment income (enjoyed mostly by the wealthy) by 22 percent. Meanwhile, to make up the difference, payroll taxes on Social Security and Medicare have risen: in the immediate postwar years, Social Security hovered around 10 percent of Federal revenue, but it grew to 40 percent by 2003. This means that America has transferred wealth to the upper-income brackets by shifting taxation from corporations and the rich onto the paychecks of middle- and lower-income groups.

And as the federal government gives up revenue sources, it shifts expenses onto the states, who must react with budget cuts. The result: we don't have the money to build schools or pay teachers and police. In the name of a narrowly conceived individual liberty to maximize profit, public institutions which support *all* are being gutted.

◆

Until November 2004, Oregon stood against this destructive tide of privatizing and narrow individualism. Oregonians turned back direct attempts to repeal Oregon's land-use laws several times; opinion polls that ask about it find "strong bipartisan support." But Measure 37 passed by 60 percent statewide.

Even progressive Multnomah County passed it. Comprising the east-side half of Portland, this is one of the most left-leaning communities in the United States. It believes so strongly in government that it helped create that *additional* layer of regional Metro government for itself. It passed an added local income tax to support schools and trounced an attempted repeal. It supported John Kerry for president by an amazing 72 percent. And yet it also affirmed Measure 37 by 51.5 percent.

Why? One reason is that the half-truth of Measure 37's "fairness" language packaged this bill in a way that seemingly no electorate could pass up. Success was guaranteed when the state Attorney General's office approved ballot language that failed to mention the other half of the truth—that while a few lucky owners would profit, their neighbors and communities as a whole would suffer.

Almost daily now, post-election news stories recount consequences of which voters were probably unaware. Pear orchards in Hood River being prepared for subdivision. House building at Wallowa Lake that will encroach on Chief Joseph's gravesite and ring the beautiful lake with development. Three hundred acres of Yamhill County farmland apparently destined to be built out. Neighbors are waking up, communities are organizing, but it may be too late. As usual, the individualism of the private-property owner—this too-narrow vision of "fairness"—simply means: *let someone else pay the price.*

But it is not only the bad luck of ballot-title wording that accounts for this backlash against Oregon's land-use system. There's a deeper problem. The anti-regulation campaign employed a locally famous, elderly widow— Dorothy English—who had been trying since the 1970s to subdivide her land in Portland's West Hills. Her story encapsulated the complaint of unfairness, of government "taking" a private individual's wealth and thumbing its bureaucratic nose at attempts for redress. This is the emotional heart of the "takings" controversy found throughout the West. And what pro-regulation forces have failed to notice is that there actually is an obvious and pressing fairness issue to be solved in such cases.

But instead of response and redress, there has been a four-year failure by politicians to respond—a collapse of leadership. The disaster-and-reprieve of the similar Measure 7 in 2000 ought to have been a sufficient warning that something needed to be done; but legislative attempts at compromise folded, a bill to specifically compensate Dorothy English was vetoed by the governor, and in the end, Oregon's leaders responded to concerns about fairness by doing nothing. Even Portland's local Metro government did astonishingly little to respond to Measure 7 *or* Measure 37.

◆

I believe a fortress mentality had grown up, among progressives, along the borders of the UGB. The Oregon Supreme Court ruling against Measure 7 only reinforced a dangerous head-in-the-sand response. Meanwhile the land-use system had, it seems, hardened into an opaque bureaucratic tangle that could neither make sense to citizens who interacted with it, nor respond adequately even to the most vivid challenges in the voting booth.

Metro, for instance, overseeing the populous territory of greater Portland, can often hardly explain its own actions. I have already told part of the story of the man I met in Gresham with his few acres of nursery land, excluded from urban development by a zig-zag in the UGB. Why the zig-zag? He asked; no one knew. No one—not even the Metro councilor I was walking with that day—could explain it. It meant a few hundred thousand to him. It remained a Kafkaesque mystery.

It seemed to echo the complaints of Kathy Iburg and Gary Conkling, whose frustrated attempts to develop a genuine new-urbanist, smart-growth plan on that city-surrounded parcel called Reed's Crossing is described elsewhere in this book. Iburg told me, on the day we walked it: "Mike Burton [then-President of Metro] said: 'If this isn't an example of the insanity of our land-use laws, I don't know what is!' I was sitting in the audience—I heard him say it."

Metro's answer was to create a huge expansion of the UGB, not in a place like Reed's Crossing, already surrounded by urban infrastructure, but in far Damascus. Why? I have heard a Metro official admit what Iburg suspected: that the whole idea of expanding into Damascus was to *delay* development. It was far easier, politically, to push the problem out there, than face NIMBY neighbors in Reed's Crossing opposed to any change, however reasonable.

The act of drawing a line on a map seems, for many progressive Portlanders, to be an invitation to fortress thinking: an attempt to forestall change and avoid the hard, community-building work of balancing, case by case, private fairness and public interest. The "managing growth" purpose of the UGB all too easily lapses into a "preventing growth" mode. That was not our community compact.

One more example. Just weeks before the fatal vote, Metro government seemed belatedly to be getting the message about its heavy-handedness and aloofness. To avoid sweeping environmental restrictions (called Goal Five measures) that were about to be imposed, a number of landowners had chainsawed hundreds of their own trees over the summer. Obviously, they regarded the prospective measures as impossibly onerous. Then, in October Metro offered what its officers called "one of the most significant changes in a decade or more"—reversing course from hard-and-fast rule enforcement to a "gentler" mixture of public education, restoration, and buy-outs. With the gun of Measure 37 to its head, Metro finally responded. But a citizen could rightly ask: Why not take this approach from the beginning? Why wait until one month before the election?

Those tree-cutting landowners may have been mistaken about the new restrictions. I wouldn't want to assume the Goal Five measures weren't good ones. And there's an important discussion to be had about America's addiction to continual economic growth, too. But my point is about perception. And perception of fairness, in a democracy, is not a trivial consideration. It goes to the consent of the governed. It is the stuff of which community, and democracy, are actually made.

What should a citizen of a democracy think about a system which seems immune to logic, above explanation, and insulated from individual citizens' rights, complaints, or questions? Answer: Apparently, citizens get mad and demand change. And that's what has happened.

Democracy is like a name written on the water. It is a process, not a fortress, and thus is always up for grabs. The meaning of the process is inclusion, consent, a sense of fairness.

◆

The disaster of Measure 37 can be turned into a paradoxical victory if it is grasped as an opportunity to *get it right*—to put land-use laws on a footing that most citizens will support. This will mean reckoning with the understandable desires of landowners to know, and to be able to predict, what their fate will be. This will mean progressives will have to go to work reminding, convincing, gathering coalitions in favor of the beautiful community we always said we were trying to build.

Perhaps something like what biologists call "adaptive management" will be called for—a more flexible style, not oriented toward "compliance," but toward results . . . with an openness to adjusting as you go (much like what Iburg and Conkling were calling for). Douglas Kelbaugh captures the essential reason this may be needed:

> . . . because city making is among the most complex and difficult human undertakings—as complex as life itself. It is beyond the powers of rational analysis and synthesis. Like civilization or language, cities cannot be invented in one generation. They must be designed and built incrementally, evolving slowly and laboriously ... And, like any self-regulating system, they must correct and recorrect themselves continuously.

It is as if a city were a little wildness, an organism of amazing intricacy that calls for humility, flexibility . . . not *plannerizing*, to use my grumpy word. And Metro President David Bragdon seems to be heading in this direction. In his 2005 "State of the Region" speech, he acknowledged "that we need to reform some of those systems" that had recently been challenged by voters:

> That doesn't mean repudiating all the good things that have been done before. It does mean reforming and refreshing those systems to reflect the values that brought us this far, and changing the way we do business.

Jane Jacobs says that the spontaneous vitality of living people is the only answer to top-down, heavy-hand-of-Robert-Moses planning. If this is not to be mere anti-regulation individualism, it must mean some kind of canny, postmodern planning style, setting limits and goals but flexibly implementing them. But how? That's what Portland must invent.

We went for some thirty years on a steady course: Measures 7 and 37 will force us to correct/recorrect; to reform/refresh. In the life of a living thing, this ought to be seen as *normal*, not apocalyptic. The challenge is for us, in our time, to be as committed and creative as Republican Tom McCall, Democrat Neil Goldschmidt, and the urban-progressive/Willamette-farmer coalition were in putting the whole amazing, ambitious thing together those three decades ago.

We will have to make our vision *visible*. Metro already puts significant efforts into certain kinds of community outreach (such as the immense

2040 Growth Concept process), usually involving meetings in rooms with long tables and charts. Evidently, more is needed—maybe of a different sort. Maybe volunteers could be allowed to design signs for major arteries, announcing *You have just crossed the UGB*, with a picture, a logo, some way of projecting the excitement and success of what we're doing here. Maybe Metro government could redesign its weirdly invisible headquarters building, which, despite being a big building with a tower, turns a blank face to the Convention Center and busy Grand Avenue alongside, projecting hardly a hint of its existence. Metro and its leaders ought to consider the uses of inspiration. At present, most citizens hardly know Metro exists . . . making it quite easy to vote against what Metro stands for.

So, maybe, Metro must make itself stand for these things: A visible vision. Fair play and predictability for landowners and neighbors alike. Flexibility. And leadership: standing up, in public, to propose, take flak, and show the way.

◆

In the democracy of water, high and low shift places continually, until the careful hierarchies of elevated and ignoble are topsy-turvied out of existence. I think of all the fragments I walked or drifted by—the wedges of neglected dampland, wetland, creek—and how surprisingly much each contributes in ecological productivity. I think of Jackson Bottom Wetlands, snug in its meander of the Tualatin River, where poopy water enters from the sewage plant at the top, and clean lakes and rivers appear at the bottom. The lowest is best here. The last shall be first. I saw geese taking off from the Wetlands' lake, mixing mud and sky indiscriminately and wanting only Thoreau or Jesus to put the parable into words.

This democracy is irresistible. Everything gets to be high eventually, and low. A man—or a goose—may eat of a fish that ate of a worm that ate of a king. And turn him into thoughts, or flights southwards, or words on paper.

In my study is a map I obtained from Metro, a topographic reconstruction of the disappeared streams of our city. We have forgotten even their names. In some sense, though, they are still running, in culverts or curbside along streets and into storm drains. Water will not stop merely because its bed is paved.

The name of the Map of Disappearing Streams seems the saddest in any language, a palimpsest of loss and waste. We each know loss and waste so many ways it ought to surprise us we have any grief to spare—yet we do.

Because the bedrock of our common life as humans and as living beings is the certainty of suffering. That is what we share, deeper than differences or creeds. No one escapes. Just as I was finishing this epilogue, an awful earth-shrugged wave in Southeast Asia killed more than two hundred thousand of our fellow humans. Then, while the book was in press, a storm washed destruction over a great American city, bringing the message home. That is the true epilogue for every political, environmental, or urban-planning discussion, the last and conclusive word.

A democracy of water is the democracy of our common flesh and common fate. Suffering, compassion, the common good. This is not a question which individualists ponder: they cannot.

That's a big thought, big as a river or a city. So I take my vision at a humbler level. Stenciled next to those subversively reappearing streams, on curbs and storm-drains around town, are little salmon-outlines, each a reminder that this water, *here*, is headed for our river, *there*. This lowly measure is my model. Direct and effective, it stimulates people daily to imagine real (though unseen) connectedness. Our job as environmentalists is always this—to remind folks of the connections: they're real, we say . . . but you need to open your mind to see them. Even disappearing streams are still here, blessing or killing salmon with your garden runoff. The air, the water, the health effects from faraway polluters. *See the connections!* is our message: *Then act!*

And in the politics of democracy, the politics of our disappearing UGB, this must also be our method, and our message. We *are* connected, and pretending otherwise—following those pied pipers of individualism and libertarianism and privatization—will be ruinous.

◆

The Boundary changed as I walked it. It's gone already, metamorphosed not just by that destructive vote but nudged and redrawn by planning decisions almost month by month. The saying is that you can never step into the same river twice. . . . So it's our turn, now, to define our community. A democracy of water cannot be saved except today.

Notes

Notes to epigraphs

Everything that is useful: Italo Calvino ("By Way of Autobiography" in *Uses of Literature,* 341)

Without community: Douglas S. Kelbaugh [(Repairing the American Metropolis, 7)

Introduction

p. 2, encapsulated: Lewis Mumford's good word, qtd. in James Howard Kunstler, *Geography of Nowhere* 10

p. 2, fatter, stupider, holier: all trends well-documented during the time of my walk.

Fatter: So many of us are obese that airlines recently announced they are considering widening their seats. Prevalence of adult American obesity reached an astounding 30.5 percent as of 2000, according to a study published in the *Journal of the American Medical Association* (Ogden et al.). This is a big jump from 22.9 percent less than one decade earlier (1988-94)(Ogden et al.), and an *astonishing* jump from 13.4 percent four decades earlier (in 1960-62) (Sharp).

Stupider: No doubt stupidness is an eternal human condition. But there are degrees. In the U.S., book-reading declined by 10 percent from 1982 to 2002, with less than half of Americans now engaged in literary reading, according to the 2004 report *Reading at Risk* by the National Endowment for the Arts. The rate of decline "has nearly tripled in the last decade." This decline bears directly on questions of civic connectedness and disconnectedness. Newspaper reading is also spiraling downwards (Angwin and Hallinan).

Meanwhile, educational levels continue at abysmal levels: the 2003 assessment of forty-one thousand students in twenty-nine countries carried out by PISA (Programme for International Student Assessment) found that American fifteen-year-olds ranked about twenty-fourth in math, science, and problem-solving— right behind economic backwaters like Latvia and Hungary—and only slightly better in reading. The U.S. showed no statistically meaningful improvement in any category since the 2000 assessment (OECD/PISA). So it can be no big surprise that about half of all college students now need remedial courses in math and reading, according to the U.S. Department of Education (Williams).

As measurable stupidness increases, disaffected, go-it-alone hyper-individualism increases. Perhaps there's a causal relation? Less reading, less information, less understanding ... leads to more disconnection, more anger, more dismantling of public services and education ... a vicious circle.

Holier: ... should of course be written "holier" because I'm really referring to an increase in *public* godliness, which is usually the opposite of the real thing. According to the continuing "World Values Survey" conducted since 1981, citizens in the U.S. *claim* a higher level of church attendance than any other first-world country: 44 percent, as compared to typical European levels in the single digits (Sweden, Norway), teens (Switzerland, West Germany), or twenties (Great Britain) (polling was done 1995-96) (Institute for Social Research and Ontario Consultants on Religious Tolerance).

However, when these numbers are cross-checked against *actual* U.S. church attendance, the real rate is around 20 percent. The study dryly summarizes: "Many Americans and Canadians tell pollsters that they have gone to church even though they have not" (Ontario Consultants on Religious Tolerance). There's actually been a slight (5 percent) decrease in U.S. churchgoing between 1981 and 1998 . . . but no decrease in the declared "importance of God in [my] life" (Inglehart and Baker, 46-47). According to Thorleif Pettersson's report derived from the World Values Survey, U.S. public religiosity places it in the disturbing company of Ukraine, South Africa, and the Philippines (10).

The figures thus support what common sense already knows: hypocrisy always accompanies public religiosity. The belligerent public fundamentalism of right-wing politics both feeds on and exacerbates our increasing ignorance, maleducation, and alienation, another part of the vicious cycle.

p. 3, official UGB Website: "Oregon's Nineteen Statewide Planning Goals and Guidelines"—the official criteria that govern the local UGBs are on the Land Conservation and Development Commission website: www.lcd.state.or.us/LCD/goals.shtml. Metro government site is www.metro-region.org.

p. 3, To administer: Metro was created in 1978; before that, the UGB was managed by CRAG (Columbia Region Association of Governments). Metro's self description: "Metro protects open space and parks, plans for land use and transportation, and manages garbage disposal and recycling for 1.3 million residents in three counties and 25 cities in the Portland, Oregon, region" (Metro) Metro government also owns and manages the Oregon Zoo, Convention Center, Expo Center, and Performing Arts Center.

p. 3, LCDC: As if to maximize confusion, this *commission* is the governing body for the larger *department* called DLCD. It would be safe to say few citizens know what either one is. This wonkish impenetrability is the bureaucratic style that has alienated many Oregonians, perhaps even those who support planning. It's called "smart growth" but we often find ourselves dumbfounded by it.

p. 3, habitually refer to it . . . example of the "New Urbanism": for instance Peter Calthorpe's regional overview in Peter Katz, *The New Urbanism* (xii); or Kunstler's use of Portland as a contrast to the usual awful planning: "Portland . . . embodies the most hopeful and progressive trends in American city life and especially in urban planning" (189).

p. 4, Like all utopias, it could be about to vanish: Oregonians passed

Measure 37 in November 2004, substantially overturning the entire system (discussed at length below, in the Epilogue). A lawsuit at the end of 2005 won a temporary stay, buut the measure was upheld by the state Supreme Court in February 2006. Other challenges include one in 1982, when developers mounted their *third* statewide initiative against the land-use planning system, and would have won it—except for ex-governor Tom McCall's inspired leadership, literally from his deathbed (Walth 452-69).

p. 4, Lucy Lippard: *The Lure of the Local* 48.

p. 4, Douglas Kelbaugh: *Repairing the American Metropolis* 13-14.

Distance from the Center

p. 13, Linda K. Johnson: did a series of dances on selected places along the UGB in the summer of 1999. It was part of a comprehensive show of gallery art and installations about the UGB called "Spanning Boundaries: Portland Metropolitan's Urban Growth Boundary" sponsored by Orlo, "a nonprofit organization exploring environmental issues through the creative arts" (Orlo).

The John Muir Reappearances

These ghost-walked chapters offer my best attempt to accurately paraphrase and summarize the guest's views. Since they are in the form of conversations, I have silently mixed paraphrase with direct quotes. Exact sources for quotes are always given. But a writer's ideas are often developed over decades in multiple

books and articles, so sources for paraphrases are representative, not exhaustive. Complete citations are in the Works Cited.

Key to Sources:

John Muir:

 Badé: *Life and Letters of John Muir*, 2 Vols., Ed. William Frederic Badé (1923)

 FO: "The Forests of Oregon and their Inhabitants" (1888) in ST

 FW: "The Forests of Washington" (1888) in ST

 LJ: *John Muir's Last Journey: South to the Amazon and East to Africa*, Ed. Michael P. Branch (2001)

 MC: *The Mountains of California* (1894)

 MFS: *My First Summer in the Sierra* (1911)

 PCO: "The Physical and Climatic Characteristics of Oregon" (1888) in ST

 ST: *Steep Trails* (1918)

Other sources:

 Cohen: *The Pathless Way: John Muir and American Wilderness*, Michael P. Cohen

 Jordan: *The Days of a Man: Being Memories of a Naturalist, Teacher, and Minor Prophet of Democracy*, 2 Vols., David Starr Jordan

 Turner: *John Muir: Rediscovering America*, Frederick Turner

 DO: *Daily Oregonian*, Portland, Oregon

p. 27, well-tilled field: FW 227.

p. 27, risking a sharp fight: See Mary Louise Swett to Louie Wanda Strentzel, 8 April 1880, Badé ii.132.

p. 27, paragraphs: DO 17 and 19 January 1880

p. 27, review: DO 13 January 1880.

p. 27, war in Afghanistan . . .
Democrats: DO January 13 and 17,
1880.

p. 27, Portland at our feet: PCO 292.

p. 27, desolation . . . far-reaching
harmonies: a continuous motif in
Muir—these phrases from MC 47,
54.

p. 28, Nature all lavish . . . building,
pulling down: MFS 238

p. 28, seems enormous waste: MFS
242-43.

p. 28, beneath all the woods: FO 311.

p. 28, Godful: a favorite turn of
phrase; see for instance the "Godful
wilderness" MFS 241 or a good spot
"where one might hope to see God"
MFS 49.

p. 29, thrush: LJ 26

p. 29, howling metropolis: Badé ii.117.

p. 29, all good in a food and shelter
way: Badé ii.217.

p. 29, eternal unfitness of civilized
things: Badé ii.121

p. 29, metropolitan evils: Badé ii.118

p. 29, all . . . more or less sick: qtd. in
Cohen 217

p. 29, there is no daylight . . . the
weary public ought to know: qtd. in
Cohen 218.

p. 29, Mt. Hood: PCO 295. The friend
is probably the artist William Keith,
with whom Muir returned to the
northwest for extensive travels in
1888.

p. 30, steel, not iron: Muir does not
identify the bridge, but the Steel
Bridge was new in 1888 when he
visited; the present "Steel Bridge" is
its modern replacement, according
to the Portland Oregon Visitors
Association; see also Sharon Wood
Wortman, *The Portland Bridge Book*.

p. 30, the glory of the country: PCO
293

p. 30, Oh look . . . repose and beauty:
PCO 296-97.

p. 30, Jordan: David Starr Jordan, first
president of Stanford University,
Badé ii.127

p. 30, I never got on: Jordan admired
Muir's writing, but there's a note
of condescension in his response
to the man himself—calling him
"simple-hearted and enthusiastic"
i.217, but also the "priest of
the High Sierra" i.459; cf Badé
ii.127, ii.130, and cp Cohen, who
comments Jordan was "too
conservative to like Muir's wilder
sort of writing" 242.

p. 30, sordid work: Turner lists some
of Muir's complaints about ranch
life, 276

p. 30, I saw your forests: Turner
comments "it was the forests of
Oregon that truly released him,"
274.

p. 30, climbed Rainier without really
meaning to: Badé ii.219.

p. 30, started writing again: while in
Oregon in 1888, Muir received a
pivotal letter from his wife Louie,
urging him to return to his "noble
life" as a wilderness advocate—
which he did: Badé ii.220.

p. 30, Mount Jordan: It was officially
named by the Sierra Club in
1925, according to Erwin Gudde,
California Place Names; but Jordan
reports that the mountaineer (and
professor) Bolton Coit Brown had
already named it thus on his maps
by 1899: Jordan i.650.

p. 30, too brushy: Jordan i.650.

P. 30, (Actually it had scared me half
to death: My Mt. Jordan story is at
the end of *Earth Rising*.

p. 31, ice and granite: qtd. in Turner
243.

p. 31, only a few inches: FO 323-24. Chickaree is the other name for this tiny squirrel.

p. 31, We little know: MC 50

p. 31, An evangel: MC 47

p. 31, Even these clouds . . . plash of rain: LJ 43

p. 31, Umbellifera: Muir habitually references botanical families to identify, here using the older term for plants of the parsnip family, like the familiar Queen Anne's Lace.

p. 31, between every two pines: a famous yet hard-to-trace Muir quotation.

Boots on the Ground in Sherwood Forest

p. 32, twenty thousand civilians: A more likely estimate, a year later, placed the civilian dead at 100,000 (Roberts et al.). See Lila Guterman's analysis of the American public's determined ignoring of both these facts and this story, in *The Chronicle of Higher Education* (Guterman).

p. 32, "Rise free from care": Thoreau *Walden* ("Baker Farm") 158.

p. 34, Many more of these folks, poorer . . . will have enlisted: The National Priorities Project reported in November 2005 that "Nearly two-thirds of all recruits (64%) were from counties with median household incomes below the US median. . . . All of the top 20 counties had a median household income below the national median household income." The Heritage Foundation disputes the conclusions—but not the numbers (Kane). An investigation undertaken by the Austen *Statesman-American* found that "Extensive Department of Defense studies from as recently as 2002 have consistently found that poor young people with low grades and the least likelihood of going to college or getting jobs are more likely to enlist, many to get college financial aid" (Castillo and Bishop). *American Prospect* reported in 2003 that only 3.5 percent of enlistees had college diplomas, with 10 percent having attended some college classes. "In demographic terms, this makes the armed forces one of the most homogeneously working-class institutions in America . . . disproportionately from blue-collar homes and neighborhoods" (Levison).

p. 36, fifty million: Geographer William M. Denevan estimates 43 to 65 million New World inhabitants in 1492 (369).

p. 37, slave labor . . . white skin: tens of thousands of American colonists in the 1600s and 1700s were *whites* kidnapped or impressed from England into often-permanent servitude in the colonies. An astonishing number were captured as children in northern England and Scotland (giving rise to the verb itself, "kid-nabbing") (Jensen 77-81).

p. 37, America is a state of mind that endures by *not-knowing*: cp R.D. Laing: "In order to rationalize our military-industrial complex, we have to destroy our capacity to see clearly any more what is in front of, and to imagine what is beyond, our noses" (qtd. in Jensen 61). Derrick Jensen's *The Culture of Make Believe* offers an extended examination of the roots of American power and denial.

p. 37, "I came into this world": Thoreau *Civil Disobedience* (351).

p. 38, "Under a government which imprisons any unjustly": Thoreau *Civil Disobedience* (352-53).

Neglect of "Here"

p. 43, Oh God I'm going to sound very Republican: The irony here is that it was *Republican* Governor Tom McCall who brought Oregon's land-use system into existence, and who championed it against 1980s anti-government conservatives who had very different values. Oregon had a tradition of moderate, community-conscious Republicans who contributed more than their share to Oregon's environmental and progressive legacy.

p. 44, inflamed bureaucrat mind: Here's an example. A well-known urban planner, writing in a journal whose audience is other planners and government officials, actually suggests that citizens who oppose planning shhould be labeled "terrorists" (Randolph 15).

Seemingly Paul Shepard

Key to works by Paul Shepard:

CH: *Coming Home to the Pleistocene*. Ed. Florence R. Shepard

ML: *Man in the Landscape: A Historic View of the Esthetics of Nature*

NM: *Nature and Madness*

TA: *Thinking Animals: Animals and the Development of Human Intelligence*

TC: *The Tender Carnivore and the Sacred Game*

p. 47, "always thought of [himself] as a naturalist": ML xxiii.

p. 47, Well, I'm like a little coral animal: ML xxix.

p. 47, It's a quality of attention: NM 21-22.

p. 48, When you bring home an animal: TA 11-14.

p. 48, waiting: CH 47.

p. 48, normal killing: CH 4.

p. 48, incarnate as natural forms: CH 169.

p. 48, our own creatures within, TA 14.

pp. 48-49, "the other" . . . not entirely assimilable, CH 145.

p. 49, a participant and receiver: ML 213.

p. 49, We've bought in to a phony dichotomy of places: CH 145.

p. 49, a subjugated natural world transcended by the human spirit: CH 4.

p. 49, The opposite of wild is not civilized but domesticated: CH 145.

p. 49, agricultural civilization is it: CH 103.

p. 49, a suite of characteristics: CH 70-77, NM and TC passim.

p. 49, the *gift*: CH 51-65.

p. 49, to feel like a crop: CH 145.

p. 49, Can you give up the city? CH 4.

p. 49, A scholar I like: Raymond Chipeniuk qtd. in CH 168.

p. 49, Exactly. Our human ecology: CH 169.

p. 50, . . . cities: NM 93-108.

p. 50, human nature . . . evolution: CH 173.

p. 50, We are Pleistocene hominids . . . edges of the wilderness: CH 137.

p. 50, Two million years: CH "Getting a Genome" 19-34.

p. 50, a light-gathering eye: see ML "The Eye" 3-27 and TA "What the Arboreal Eye Knows" 15-18.

p. 50, Our bodies and minds expect: NM 6-11 and passim.

p. 50, For most of our species life . . . in groups: NM 10; CH 45, 155, 172, etc. Shepard offers various averages for size of hunter-gatherer groups.

p. 50, **But standing cities:** CH "How we once lived" 37-66.

p. 51, **children . . . socialized as humans:** NM 93-108 and passim; CH "How the Mind Once Lived" 51-65.

p. 51, **Obviously we cannot simply re-create:** CH 173.

p. 51, *But couldn't you see Portland's experiment:* TC.

p. 51, **Maybe:** CH 107 n.50.

City Limits

page 52, farthest western point: Hillsboro is the furthest western *contiguous* UGB community. Metro also administers two nearby urban islands: Forest Grove/Cornelius (west) and Wilsonville (south).

p. 55, **50 percent of all residential zoning:** Carl Abbott, *Greater Portland: Urban Life and Landscape in the Pacific Northwest* 163.

p. 56, **the "Great Community":** John Dewey explores the concept in *The Public and its Problems* (1927).

p. 57, **briefly tried and abandoned:** Sacramento has a county "Urban Services Boundary." Sacramento talks about "smart growth" quite a bit, as *Sacramento Bee* reporter Stuart Leavenworth comments, "Yet as the Sacramento region continues to add 50,000 people a year, developers keep proposing office parks and subdivisions designed around the car, and local leaders keep approving them." The recent county-approved plan for 10,500 homes called "SunRidge" ignores transit and density concerns in favor of auto-oriented, suburban development—despite being adjacent to the new light-rail line.

p. 57, **James Howard Kunstler . . . "overwhelmingly":** *The Geography of Nowhere* 102-04.

p. 57, **Douglas Kelbaugh:** *Repairing the American Metropolis.*

p. 57, **Todd Littman:** in Alan Thein Durning, *The Car and the City* 48-50.

p. 57, **"massive transfers of wealth":** Durning 50.

p. 57, **Coleman Young:** qtd. in Lucy Leppard, *The Lure of the Local* 203.

p. 58, **"the true cost of sewer service":** Kelbaugh 31.

p. 58, **"Suburban sprawl is bankrupting":** Kelbaugh 31

p. 58, **"the tendency of interdependent . . . ":** "The Land Ethic," in Leopold's *A Sand County Almanac* 238.

p. 59, **Biologist Garret Hardin's famous essay:** "The Tragedy of the Commons" is reprinted in many sources.

p. 59, **Research since then:** See for instance Joanna Berger and Michael Gochfeld, "The Tragedy of the Commons"; Elinor Ostrom, "How Inexorable is the 'Tragedy of the Commons'?"; David Feeny et al., "The Tragedy of the Commons: Twenty-Two Years Later"; or Elinor Ostrom et al., "Revisiting the Commons: Local Lessons, Global Challenges."

p. 59, **Consider the people living here in the Northwest:** The Northwest and California were North America's most densely populated area, according to Shepard Krech III, *The Ecological Indian* 93. Michael Silverstein's overview of Chinook use of resources indicates a spectrum of control, from very tight (fishing) to "freely accessible to many surrounding groups" (root-gathering), with hunting somewhere in the middle, probably reflecting what was most (or least) valued, 536.

p. 59, **Richard White's book:** *The Organic Machine: The Remaking of the Columbia River.*

p. 59, **"an almost endless list . . ."** Rubin 17. These taboos and requirements are visible, for example, in the "Coyote Myth" collected by Franz Boas from Chinook-speaker Charles Cultee in 1890-91 (9-21).

p. 59, **Most . . . "commons" are regulated:** "No such simple commons has ever operated. It never existed on the Columbia": White 39-40.

p. 59, **Stories . . . myths:** See White 18-19, 100; Rubin 17-18; Boas.

p. 60, **Call it the fallacy of choice in a vacuum:** "What is the use of a house if you haven't got a tolerable planet to put it on?" asked Thoreau in a letter to H. G. O. Blake in May of 1860 (qtd. in Philippon 166 n. 4).

p. 60, **"Democracy was born of . . . conscience":** John Berger, "The Soul and the Operator," 575.

p. 61, **only within limits:** Novelist and art critic Jeanette Winterson (in the words of a character): "The paradox is that the artificial and often mechanical nature of the rules produces inexhaustible freedom." *Art and Lies* 139.

Reed's Crossing

p. 63, **nineteen planning goals:** Goal Three states "Agricultural lands shall be preserved and maintained for farm use" (Oregon DLCD).

p. 64, **1000 Friends of Oregon actively opposed:** The case against Reed's Crossing is summarized by Mary Kyle McCurdy, Staff Attorney for 1000 Friends of Oregon: "The main, and significant, difference between the two areas is that St. Mary's [i.e. the Reed's Crossing parcel] is all farm land (and great farm land, at that, with drainage, in one ownership, and a large parcel). And Damascus is not farm land—most, if not all, of it was already zoned for rural residential use. Nine thousand people already live in the community of Damascus, while the St. Mary's/Newland parcel is uninhabited and in agricultural production. Damascus was facing the slow choking of incremental suburbanization. Including it in the UGB is now providing that area with a unique opportunity to build a community, reflected in the fact that the Damascus area recently incorporated as a city to take charge of its future. Washington County is the third most productive agricultural county in the state, and produces a wide diversity of crops. State law requires that land zoned for farming or forestry be last in line to be brought into a UGB."

p. 64, **Clackamas County zoning map:** technically the "Damascus/Boring Concept Plan"; as calculated by Tim O'Brien at Metro Data Resource Center, exclusive timber and agricultural zoning comprised only about 3565 acres of the 12,000 acre Damascus expansion area, while the single largest zoning category was "RRFF5" or "rural residential farm forest 5 acre."

p. 66, **"exception land":** defined by Metro as "Land next to the urban growth boundary that is not farm or forest," second in priority for being brought inside the UGB (after first-priority "urban reserve land" designated for future growth) (Metro *Guidelines for bringing land into the UGB*).

Doublewides in Ecotopia

p. 73, Anna Bermingham: Along with the picturesque came a new vogue of landscape painting in the 1780s, followed by the whole Romantic Movement in poetry. *Landscape and Ideology: The English Rustic Tradition 1740-1860* 1, 9, passim.

p. 73, not at all: "Not at all" is perhaps a too-sweeping rhetorical flourish. Wendell Berry, Richard White, Kirkpatrick Sale, Morris Berman, and many others have written about class, work, economics, and sociology in relation to ecology and environmentalism. But I'm sticking with my flourish, because I do not see that their efforts have significantly shifted the environmental movement's attention onto questions of people and work.

p. 74, "magnitude of need for more affordable housing": Metro *Land-use planning,* "Affordable Housing"; **Goal 10:** Oregon Department of Land Conservation and Development (DLCD), "Oregon's 19 Statewide Planning Goals and Guidelines."

p. 75, There's abundant bureaucratic machinery: A Metro ordinance of 18 January 2001 requires "all cities and counties" to amend their Comprehensive Plans and report to Metro on how they have pursued affordable housing (Metro *Land-use planning,* "Affordable Housing"). But continuing delays seem to indicate the machinery of twenty-four local governments creaking ponderously into action, "considering" various

actions and writing "compliance reports" to Metro about them (Metro, *Urban Growth Management Functional Plan Annual Compliance Report* [Revised February 5, 2004]).

p. 75, "artificial shortage of buildable land": John A. Charles of the Cascade Policy Institute, a free-market, libertarian-leaning Oregon think tank.

p. 75, The home-builder/libertarian makes a common-sense case: In their very thoroughgoing critique, for instance, Staley, Edgens, and Mildner can only point to a "*potential* impact . . . on housing prices" (Part 3: "Growth Boundaries and Housing Affordability"). Or they use a future tense that shows the point is a prediction, not an observed phenomenon: "as land becomes less and less available inside the growth boundary, land owners *will* be able to charge higher prices . . . when housing demand is strong since they *will* have less competition" ("Appendix A: Vacant Land, Developable Land, and Redevelopment") (emphasis added in both quotes).

p. 75, But when this assumption is tested: See Justin Phillips and Eban Goodstein, "Growth Management and Housing Prices: The Case of Portland, Oregon." According to evaluations of other researchers, Philips and Goodstein used appropriately skeptical "worst-case" methodology: Arthur C. Nelson et al. 26.

p. 75, "only about average for Western cities": using eight other Western cities of over one-million population for comparison (Phillips and Goodstein).

p. 75, less than $10,000: (Phillips and Goodstein). A study published two years later came to "essentially the same conclusion using different approaches" (qtd. in Nelson et al. 26). Phillips and Goodstein's less-likely worst-case analysis says the UGB might add as much as 7 percent to the median housing price.

p. 75, median home price: the National Association of Home Builders (NAHB) "Housing Opportunity Index" for first quarter of 2002. The NAHB thereafter ceased publishing this data.

Cities above one-million population *on the West Coast*:

	Median price	Affordability
San Francisco	$525,000	9.2%
San Jose	451,000	20.1
San Diego	290,000	21.6
Los Angeles	240,000	34.4
Seattle	234,000	63.1
Sacramento	218,000	43.7
Riverside (CA)	167,000	49.6
Portland	167,000	46.6
(NAHB)		

p. 76, singled out for their sprawl: *Riverside* is named the worst by the "Smart Growth America" advocacy group; *Sacramento* is singled out by Robert W. Wassmer in *Urban sprawl in a U.S. metropolitan area: Ways to measure and a comparison of the Sacramento area to similar metropolitan areas in California and the U.S.* (2000).

p. 76, So much for government regulations artificially running up the price: Other research has been appearing that reinforces this conclusion. See essays in Anthony Downs, ed., *Growth Management and Affordable Housing: Do They Conflict?*; and Deborah Howe, "The Reality of Portland's Housing Market" in Ozawa, ed., *The Portland Edge.*

p. 76, "desirability": See conclusion of Nelson et al.: "In the context of strong housing demand, growth management can adversely affect housing affordability by making the community even more desirable— which is, after all, its intent" (36).

p. 76, Oregon's worst-in-the-nation unemployment rate: Oregon state economist Art Ayre states that unemployment in Oregon (along with that of Alaska) rated worst or second-worst for the thirty-nine months ending in December 2004 (Chuang).

p. 76, city's population grew ... 1.7 percent: U.S. Census Bureau, "Annual Estimate of Population for Incorporated Places in Oregon," (2004).

p. 76, Seattle, by comparison, grew ... 1 percent: City Demographer Diana Cornelius (2004).

p. 76, Portland ranks high: in a ten-year study by Joseph Cortwright and Carol Coletta (Cortwright).

p. 76, Richard Florida: His recent books that focussed attention on the importance of cities attracting young, creative talent include *Cities and the Creative Class* and *The Rise of the Creative Class: And How It's Transforming Work, Leisure, Community and Everyday Life.*

p. 76, Portland ... Sacramento: Cortwright and Coletta rank the top fifty metro areas, measuring rate of change in population of twenty-five- to thirty-four-year olds with four-year degrees (Sacramento is forty-first).

p. 76, 31 percent . . . fifty-one thousand jobs . . . five times as many: Metro. *Metro Regional Data Book, Portland-Vancouver Metropolitan Area*: 101-02.

p. 77, While Vancouver has finally begun to develop some improved planning: Vancouver has been doing better lately—developing a more distinctive downtown, more density, and stronger planning. But Clark County is moving in the other direction, taking fast-growth decisions Vancouver is not in accord with, according to officials in the Vancouver Long Range Planning Department (Hudson; Snodgrass). Clark County recently even fired a planning manager who dared voice criticism of the sprawling pro-growth agenda (Middlewood).

Italo Calvino Invisibly Key:

Auto: "By Way of an Autobiography" in *Uses*

Cosmi: *Cosmicomics*

Cyber: "Cybernetics and Ghosts" in *Uses*

Invisible: *Invisible Cities*

Levels: "Levels of Reality in Literature" in *Uses*

Lit: "Literature as Projection of Desire: On Northrop Frye's *Anatomy of Criticism*" in *Uses*

MP: *Mr. Palomar*

6Mem: *Six Memos for the Next Millennium*

Uses: *The Uses of Literature: Essays*

Utopia: "On Fourier, III: Envoi: A Utopia of Fine Dust" in *Uses*

p. 84, To walk abroad using the imagination: *6Mem* 97.

p. 84, para-utopian activity: Utopia 250.

p. 84, Well, there ought to be a loophole left for incompleteness: *6Mem* 121.

p. 85, an *open* encyclopedia: *6Mem* 116.

p. 85, model of models: *MP* 108.

p. 85, your journey created it: *Cosmi* "The Spiral" (for idea that vision creates form).

p. 85, Escher: *6Mem* 98.

p. 85, model becomes a kind of fortress: *MP* 111.

p. 85, a labyrinth . . . in which it is easy to lose oneself uses: Lit 53.

p. 85, wanderer . . . Picaro: Utopia 248 and Levels 114.

p. 85, The labyrinth . . . gain its power for himself: Cyber 25 (quoting Hans Magnus Enzensberger).

p. 85, I have always felt the call of the city, far more than my provincial roots: Auto 341.

p. 85, facsimile of the world and of society: Cyber 26.

p. 85, Everything that is useful to the whole business of living together is energy well spent: Auto 341.

p. 85, utopianism was born after the voyage of Columbus: Utopia 252.

p. 85, between history and fable: Levels 108.

p. 85, city planning: Utopia 251.

p. 85, But even if the overall design has been minutely planned: *6Mem* 116.

pp. 85-86, centrifugal force . . . a truth that is not merely partial: *6Mem* 117.

p. 86, surface of things is inexhaustible: *MP* 55.

p. 86, Soon the city fades before your eyes: *Invisible* 90.

p. 86, Like all . . . you follow zigzag lines: *Invisible* 90.

p. 86, Your footsteps follow what is within, buried, erased: *Invisible* 91.

p. 86, After all, there are many Portlands: *Invisible passim.*

p. 86, The walker's city frees itself from the driver's city, only to be replaced, exchanged: *Invisible*155.

p. 86, a temporal succession: *Invisible*163.

p. 86, At every second the unhappy city contains a happy city unaware of its own existence: *Invisible*149.

p. 86, like lovers . . . in the mirror: *Invisible* 54.

p. 86, The question made me think of walled cities, like what I saw as a child in brightly colored Sunday School pictures: *see 6Mem* 93 (the impact of comic books on his childhood imagination).

p. 87, The UGB is your frame tale: *see* Levels 116 and *Invisible passim.*

p. 87, Cities, like dreams, are made of desires and fears . . . and everything conceals something else: *Invisible* 44.

p. 88, The more enlightened our houses are, the more their walls ooze ghosts: Cyber 19.

p. 88, labyrinth: Cyber 25-26.

p. 88, What is a language vacuum if not a vestige of taboo, of a ban on mentioning something? Cyber 19.

p. 88, myth . . . the hidden part of every story, the buried part, the region that is still unexplored: Cyber 18; cf. *6Mem* 112, 119.

p. 90, different from all the habitable or uninhabitable cities of today: Utopia 252.

A View from the Vineyard

p. 91, $1.4 billion: according to a report from the Oregon Wine Board (a semi-independent state agency serving the wine industry) in January of 2006.

Epilogue: A Democracy of Water

p. 97, Lewis Thomas: Most of *Lives of a Cell* explores this irony: see for instance "On Societies as Organisms" and "On Probability and Possibility."

p. 98, Richard Epstein: Overviewed by John D. Echeverria and Raymond Booth Eby, "The Wise Use and Property Rights Movements"; for an excellent cultural analysis see John Roush's "Introduction: Freedom and Responsibility: What We Can Learn from the Wise Use Movement." A comprehensive and well-reasoned legal/cultural view of "takings" can be found in Raymond R. Coletta, "The Measuring Stick of Regulatory Takings: A Biological and Cultural Analysis."

p. 98, "Your property belongs to you": "Argument in Favor: Why buy the cow when you can get the milk for free?" *Official 2000 General Election Voters' Pamphlet* (Libertarian Party).

p. 98, "Reciprocity of advantage": A full explanation is in Andrew W. Schwartz, "Reciprocity of Advantage: the antidote to the antidemocratic trend in regulatory takings."

p. 99, Easily available tax facts: See for instance Robert Greenstein and Isaac Shapiro, "The New, Definitive CBO Data on Income and Tax Trends."

p. 99, 1943 corporations paid 40 percent . . . 7.4 percent: Warren Vieth.

p. 99, Tax rates . . . dropping: Citizens for Tax Justice & the Institute on Taxation and Economic Policy.

p. 99, Social Security . . . 10 percent . . . 40 percent: Office of Management and Budget, 31-32.

p. 99, shifts expenses onto the states: As economist Joseph J. Minarik comments: "Unlike federal taxes, state and local taxes have increased significantly—from about 7 percent of GNP in 1954 to about 12 percent in 1991."

p. 100, "strong bipartisan support": Oregon League of Conservation Voters.

p. 100, Pear orchards: "Counting the Worms." Editorial. *Oregonian* 7 January 2005.

p. 100, Wallowa Lake: Richard Cockle, "Property rights tested at Wallowa Lake," *Oregonian* 9 January 2005.

p. 100, Three hundred acres: Laura Oppenheimer, "Measure 37 exposes nerves," *Oregonian* 2 February 2005.

p. 102, "one of the most significant changes": Laura Oppenheimer, "Metro Councilors offer Gentler Environmental Plan," *Oregonian* 14 October 2004.

p. 103, "because city making is among the most complex": Kelbaugh 48.

p. 103, David Bragdon: "2005 State of the Region Address."

p. 103, Jane Jacobs says: "[I]t is the thousands of individuals who create, by making their own choices and operating without guidance from the planners, the exciting fabric of the cosmopolitan city"

(qtd. in Lippard 245). Lucy Lippard comments further: "Given the fact that city planning has failed so miserably so often, the field itself should be scrutinized more carefully." She calls for a more humble "postmodernist planning" to stop theorizing and get to work (245). And she adds: "But we don't know how to reconstruct [cities] organically in our own contemporary image, and it's pretty clear that the artificial versions don't work" (248).

p. 103, weirdly invisible headquarters: When approaching Metro headquarters from Grand Avenue (as most citizens do), one sees not a hint of what this thing is. The workaday entrance on Grand is an example of architecture that fails to effectively demarcate human use: you can't find the entrance until you're directly in front of it. This building illustrates Metro's anonymity problem.

p. 104, how surprisingly much each contributes in ecological productivity: Dr. Laurel J. Standley of Watershed Solutions LLC (Portland) says that Portland, and several other cities, have found that one dollar invested in watershed protection "can save from $7.50 to nearly $200 for new water treatment facilities." See W.V. Reid.

Works Cited

Abbott, Carl. *Greater Portland: Urban Life and Landscape in the Pacific Northwest.* Philadelphia: University of Pennsylvania Press, 2001.

Angwin, Julia, and Joseph T. Hallinan. "Newspaper Circulation Continues Decline, Forcing Tough Decisions." *Wall Street Journal* 2 May 2005: A1.

Badé, William Frederic. *The Life and Letters of John Muir,* 2 Vols. New York: Houghton Mifflin, 1923.

Berger, Joanna, and Michael Gochfeld, "The Tragedy of the Commons." *Environment* 40 (1998): 4+.

Berger, John. "The Soul and the Operator," in *John Berger: Selected Essays.* Ed. Geoff Dryer. New York: Pantheon, 2001, 570-75.

Bermingham, Anna. *Landscape and Ideology: The English Rustic Tradition 1740-1860.* Berkeley: University of California Press, 1986.

Boas, Franz. *Chinook Texts.* Washington, D.C.: Smithsonian, 1894.

Bragdon, David. "2005 State of the Region Address." 25 January 2005. Available www.metro-region.org/article.cfm?articleID=12861.

Branch, Michael P., ed. *John Muir's Last Journey: South to the Amazon and East to Africa.* Washington, D.C.: Island Press, 2001.

Calthorpe, Peter. "The Region," in *The New Urbanism: Toward an Architecture of Community.* Ed. Peter Katz. New York: McGraw-Hull, 1994, xi-xvi.

Calvino, Italo."By Way of an Autobiography" (1980), in *The Uses of Literature,* 339-41.

———. *Cosmicomics.* Trans. William Weaver. New York: Harvest/Harcourt Brace, 1968.

———."Cybernetics and Ghosts" (1967), in *The Uses of Literature,* 3-27.

———. *Invisible Cities.* Trans. William Weaver. New York: Harvest/Harcourt Brace, 1974.

———. "Levels of Reality in Literature" (1978), in *The Uses of Literature,* 101-21.

———. "Literature as Projection of Desire: On Northrop Frye's *Anatomy of Criticism*" (1969), in *The Uses of Literature,* 50-61.

———. *Mr. Palomar.* Trans. William Weaver. New York: Harvest/Harcourt Brace, 1985.

———. "On Fourier, III: Envoi: A Utopia of Fine Dust" (1973), in *The Uses of Literature,* 245-55.

———. *Six Memos for the Next Millennium.* New York: Vintage/Random, 1993.

———. *The Uses of Literature: Essays.* Trans. Patrick Creagh. New York: Harvest/Harcourt Brace, 1986.

Castillo, Juan, and Bill Bishop. "Texas Hispanic soldiers dying at higher rate." *Austen Statesman-American,* Sunday, February 27, 2005.

Charles, John A. "Money on Portland's livability: Right conclusion, wrong reasons." *Cascade Policy Institute* 13 December 2000. Available www.cascadepolicy.org/pdf/env/moneymag.htm. Retrieved 4 November 2003.

Chuang, Angie. "Oregon growing; Economy brightens." *Oregonian* 16 November 2004: A1+.

Citizens for Tax Justice & the Institute on Taxation and Economic Policy. "Corporate Income Taxes in the Bush Years." September 2004. Available http://www.ctj.org/corpfed04an.pdf.

——— and the Institute on Taxation and Economic Policy. "Do Fat Cats Pay Lower Tax Rates than Workers?" 8 May 2004. Available www.ctj.org.

Cockle, Richard. "Property rights tested at Wallowa Lake." *Oregonian* 9 January 2005: E8.

Cohen, Michael P. *The Pathless Way: John Muir and American Wilderness.* Madison, Wisc.: University of Wisconsin Press, 1984.

Coletta, Raymond R. "The Measuring Stick of Regulatory Takings: A Biological and Cultural Analysis." University of Pennsylvania *Journal of Constitutional Law* 20 (1998). Available www.law.upenn.edu/conlaw/issues/vol1/num1/coletta/node2_ct.html. Retrieved Cannell Library 14 January 2005.

Cornelius, Diana. City Demographer, Seattle. Personal communication 16 November 2004.

Cortwright, Joseph. "Portland's New Pioneers." *Oregonian* 12 December 2004: F1+.

Daily Oregonian. "Mr. Muir's Lecture." [n.p.] 13 January 1880.

———. "Natural Science Association: Mr. Muir's Second Lecture." 17 January 1880.

———. "Mr. Muir's Lecture." [n.p.] 19 January 1880.

Denevan, William M. "The Pristine Myth: The Landscape of the Americas in 1492." *Annals of the Association of American Geographers* 82 (1992): 369-85.

Dewey, John. *The Public and its Problems* (1927). Rpt. in *The Civil Society Reader.* Eds. Virginia A Hodgkinson and Michael W. Foley. London: University Press of New England, 2003. 133-53.

Downs, Anthony, ed. *Growth Management and Affordable Housing: Do They Conflict?* Washington, D.C.: Brookings Institution, 2004.

Durning, Alan Thein. *The Car and the City.* NEW Report No. 3. Seattle: Northwest Environment Watch, 1996.

Echeverria, John D., and Raymond Booth Eby. "The Wise Use and Property Rights Movements," in *Let the People Judge: Wise Use and the Private Property Rights Movement.* Eds. John D. Echeverria and Raymond Booth Eby. Washington, D.C.: Island Press, 1995. 11-12.

Epstein, Richard A. *Takings: private property and the power of eminent domain.* Cambridge, Mass.: Harvard University Press, 1985.

Feeny, David, et al., "The Tragedy of the Commons: Twenty-Two Years Later." *Human Ecology* 18 (1990): 1-19.

Florida, Richard. *Cities and the Creative Class.* London: Routledge, 2004.

———. *The Rise of the Creative Class: And How It's Transforming Work, Leisure, Community and Everyday Life.* New York: Basic Books, 2002.

Greenstein, Robert, and Isaac Shapiro. "The New, Definitive CBO Data on Income and Tax Trends." Center on Budget and Policy Priorities, 23

September 2003. Available http://www.cbpp.org/9-23-03tax.htm.

Guterman, Lila. "Lost Count." *Chronicle of Higher Education* 4 Feb 2005: A10+. *Infotrac.* Expanded Academic ASAP. Cannell Library, 26 June 2005.

Gudde, Erwin J. *1000 California Place Names: Their Origin and Meaning.* Berkeley: University of California Press, 1959.

Hardin, Garrett. "The Tragedy of the Commons." Rpt. in *The Everlasting Universe: Readings in the Ecological Revolution.* Eds. Lorne J. Forstner and John H. Todd. Lexington, Mass.: Heath, 1971. 174-88.

Howe, Deborah. "The Reality of Portland's Housing Market." In Ozawa, ed., 184-205.

Hudson, Laura, City of Vancouver (Wash.) Long Range Planning Manager. Personal Communication, 28 June 2005.

Inglehart, Ronald, and Wayne E. Baker. "Modernization, Cultural Change, and the Persistence of Traditional Values." *World Values Survey.* Available www.worldvaluessurvey.org.

Institute for Social Research, University of Michigan. *World Values Survey.* 1999-2003. Available wvs.isr.umich.edu.

Jensen, Derrick. *The Culture of Make Believe.* New York: Context Books, 2002.

Jordan, David Starr. *The Days of a Man: Being Memories of a Naturalist, Teacher, and Minor Prophet of Democracy,* 2 Vols. Yonkers-on-Hudson, N.Y.: World, 1922.

Kane, Tim. "Is Iraq a Poor Man's War?" WebMemo #922. Heritage Foundation. Available http://www.heritage.org/Research/NationalSecurity/wm922.cfm.

Kelbaugh, Douglas S. *Repairing the American Metropolis.* Seattle: University of Washington Press, 2002.

Krech, Shepard, III. *The Ecological Indian.* New York: Norton, 1999.

Kunstler, James Howard. *The Geography of Nowhere: The Rise and Decline of America's Man-Made Landscape.* New York: Simon and Schuster, 1993.

Libertarian Party of Oregon. "Argument in Favor: Why buy the cow when you can get the milk for free?" *Official 2000 General Election Voters' Pamphlet. Vol. 1:*

Measures. Oregon: Secretary of State, November 7, 2000. 315.

Leavenworth, Stuart. "Grappling with Growth: Planners' Dreams vs. Developers' Reality." *Sacramento Bee* 9 December 2001. Available www.sacbee. com/content/news/projects/v-print/ story/1293936pc.html. Retrieved 10 February 2005.

Leopold, Aldo. *A Sand County Almanac.* New York: Ballantine, 1966.

Levison, Andrew. "Class and Warfare: Democrats and the rhetoric of patriotism." *American Prospect* September 2003.

Lippard, Lucy R. *The Lure of the Local: Senses of Place in a Multicentered Society.* New York: New Press, 1997.

McCurdy, Mary Kyle, Staff Attorney. 1000 Friends of Oregon. Personal communications 28 June 2005 and 13 July 2005.

Metro. www.metro-region.org.

———. *Guidelines for bringing land into the UGB.* www.metro-region.org/article. cfm?ArticleID=280

———. *Land-use planning.* "Affordable Housing." www.metro-region.org/ article.cfm?articleid=269.

———. *Metro Regional Data Book, Portland-Vancouver Metropolitan Area.* Metro Data Resource Center, January 2005: 101-02. www.metro-region.org/ library_docs/maps_data/metroregional databookjan2005.pdf.

———. *Urban Growth Management Functional Plan Annual Compliance Report.* (Revised February 5, 2004). www.metro-region.org/library_docs/ land_use/2003_annual_compliance_ report.pdf.

Middlewood, Erin. "Top long-range planner removed; County board objects to report critical of liftint 'hold' on growth." *Columbian* 24 June 2005: A1. *ProQuest.* Cannell Library. 28 June 2005.

Minarik, Joseph J. "Taxation, a Preface." *The Concise Encyclopedia of Economics.* Available http://www.econlib.org/ library/Enc/TaxationAPreface.html.

Muir, John. "The Forests of Oregon and their Inhabitants" (1888), in *Steep Trails,* 299-326.

———."The Forests of Washington" (1888), in *Steep Trails,* 227-47.

———. *The Mountains of California* (1894). San Francisco: Sierra Club Books, 1988.

———. *My First Summer in the Sierra* (1911). Boston: Houghton Mifflin, 1979.

———."The Physical and Climatic Characteristics of Oregon" (1888), in *Steep Trails,* 271-98.

———. *Steep Trails.* Ed. William Frederic Badé. New York: Houghton Mifflin, 1923.

National Association of Home Builders (NAHB). "Housing Opportunity Index" [first quarter, 2002]. www.NAHB.org. Retrieved 18 October 2004.

National Endowment for the Arts. "Literary Reading in Dramatic Decline, According to National Endowment for the Arts Survey." *National Endowment for the Arts News Room,* 8 July 2004. www.nea.gov/news/news04/ ReadingAtRisk.html.

National Priorities Project. "Military Recruitment in FY2004." November 1, 2005. Available http://nationalpriorities. org/index.php?option=com_content&t ask=view&id=177&Itemid=107.

Nelson, Arthur C., et al., "The Link Between Growth Management and Housing Affordability: The Academic Evidence." Discussion Paper for Center on Urban and Metropolitan Policy. Brookings Institution, February 2002.

Oates, David. *Earth Rising: Ecological Belief in an Age of Science.* Corvallis, Ore.: Oregon State University Press, 1989.

O'Brien, Tim. Senior Regional Planner, Metro Planning Department. Personal Communication 28 December 2005.

OECD/PISA. Organisation for Economic Co-operation and Development/ Programme for International Student Assessment . *Learning for Tomorrow's World –First Results from PISA 2003.* "Executive Summary." Available www. pisa.oecd.org.

Office of Management and Budget. *Budget of the United States Government, Fiscal Year 2005,* "Historical Tables" Table 2.2. 31-32.

Ogden, Dr. Cynthia L., et al., "Prevalence and Trends in Obesity Among US Adults, 1999-2000." *Journal of the American Medical Association* 288 (2002): 1723-27.

Ontario Consultants on Religious Tolerance. "How Many People Go Regularly to Weekly Religious Services?" 26 Nov 2001.www.religioustolerance. org.

Oppenheimer, Laura. "Measure 37 exposes nerves." *Oregonian* 2 February 2005: C1.

————. "Metro Councilors offer Gentler Environmental Plan." *Oregonian* 14 October 2004: D1.

Oregon Department of Land Conservation. "Oregon's 19 Statewide Planning Goals and Guidelines." www. lcd.state.or.us/LCD/goals.shtml.

Oregon Land Conservation and Development Commission. www.lcd. state.or.us/LCD/lcdc.shtml.

Oregon League of Conservation Voters. *The 2001 Environmental Handbook for the Oregon Legislature.* "Chapter 13: Land Use Planning." 2001. Available http://www.olcv.org/handbook/chap13. html.

Oregonian. "Counting the Worms." Editorial. 7 January 2005: E8.

Oregon Wine Board. *The Economic Impact of the Wine and Wine Grape Industries on the Oregon Economy.* Jan. 2006. Available www.oregonwine.org.Orlo. www.orlo.org.

Ostrom, Elinor. "How Inexorable is the 'Tragedy of the Commons?' Institutional Arrangements for Changing the Structure of Social Dilemmas." Distinguished Faculty Research Lecture. Bloomington, Ind.: Indiana University, Office of the Vice President, Bloomington Office of Research and Graduate Development, 1986.

————, et al. "Revisiting the Commons: Local Lessons, Global Challenges." *Science* 9 April 1999: 278-82.

Ozawa, Connie P., ed. *The Portland Edge: Challenges and Successes in Growing Cities.* Washington, D.C.: Island Press, 2004.

Pettersson, Thorleif. "The Relations between Religion and Politics in the Contemporary Western World: The impact of secularization, postmodernization and peoples' basic value orientations." *World Values Survey.* Available www.worldvaluessurvey.org.

Philippon, Daniel J. "Edward Abbey's remarks at the Cracking of Glen Canyon Dam." *ISLE* 11.2 (2004): 161-66.

Phillips, Justin, and Eban Goodstein. "Growth Management and Housing Prices: The Case of Portland, Oregon." *Contemporary Economic Policy* 18 (2000): 334+.

Portland Oregon Visitors Association. www.travelportland.com.

Randolph, Hester. "Life Liberty and the Pursuit of Sustainable Happiness." *Places* 9 (Winter 1995): 4-17.

Reid, W. V. (no title). In *Managing Human Dominated Ecosystems.* Eds. G. Chichilnisky et al. Monographs in Systematic Botany Vol. 84. St. Louis: Missouri Botanical Garden, 2001. 197-255.

Roberts, Les, et al. "Mortality before and after the 2003 invasion of Iraq: cluster sample survey." *The Lancet* 364 (Nov 20, 2004): 1857+. *Infotrac.* Expanded Academic ASAP. Cannell Library, 26 June 2004.

Roush, John. "Introduction: Freedom and Responsibility: What We Can Learn from the Wise Use Movement," in *Let the People Judge: Wise Use and the Private Property Rights Movement.* Eds. John D. Echeverria and Raymond Booth Eby. Washington, D.C.: Island Press, 1995. 1-10. Rubin, Rick. *Naked Against the Rain: The People of the Lower Columbia 1770-1830.* Portland: Far Shore, 1999.

Schwartz, Andrew W. "Reciprocity of advantage: The antidote to the antidemocratic trend in regulatory takings." *UCLA Journal of Environmental Law* 22 (2004): 1-76.

Sharp, David W. "Americans Are Getting Fatter—and They Are Not Alone." *Science Watch* March/April 2004: 5. Available www.sciencewatch.com/ march-april2004/sw_march-april2004_ page5.htm.

Shepard, Paul. *Coming Home to the Pleistocene.* Ed. Florence R. Shepard. Washington, D.C.: Island Press, 1998.

———. *Man in the Landscape: A Historic View of the Esthetics of Nature* (1967). Athens, Ga.: University of Georgia Press, 2002.

———. *Nature and Madness.* San Francisco: Sierra Club, 1982.

———. *Thinking Animals: Animals and the Development of Human Intelligence* (1978). Athens, Ga.: University of Georgia Press, 1998.

———. *The Tender Carnivore and the Sacred Game.* New York: Scribners, 1973.

Silverstein, Michael. "Chinookans of the Lower Columbia," in *Handbook of North American Indians*, Vol. 7 Northwest Coast. Ed. Wayne Suttles. Washington, D.C.: Smithsonian, 1990. 533-46.

Smart Growth America. www. smartgrowthamerica.org/sprawlindex.

Snodgrass, Bryan, City of Vancouver (Wash.) Principal Planner, Comprehensive Plan and Sub-area Planning. Personal communication 28 June 2005.

Soon, Yan, and Gerrit-Jan Knaap. "Measuring Urban Form: Is Portland Winning the War on Sprawl?" *Journal of the American Planning Association* 70 (Spring 2004): 212.

Staley, Samuel R., Jefferson G. Edgens, and Gerard C. S. Mildner. *A Line in the Sand: Urban-Growth Boundaries, Smart Growth, and Housing Affordability.* Reason Public Policy Institute (RPPI), Policy Study No. 263. November 1999. Available www.rppi.org/urban/ps263. html. Retrieved 20 November 2004.

Standley, Laurel J., Ph. D. Managing Director, Watershed Solutions, LLC. Personal communication 1 Feb 2005.

Thomas, Lewis. *Lives of a Cell* (1974). New York: Penguin, 1978.

Thoreau, Henry David. *The Variorum Civil Disobedience,* in *Walden and Civil Disobedience: The Variorum Editions.* Ed. Walter Harding. New York: Washington Square, 1967. 325-68.

———. *The Variorum Walden,* in *Walden and Civil Disobedience: The Variorum*

Editions. Ed. Walter Harding. New York: Washington Square, 1967. 1-321.

Turner, Frederick. *John Muir: Rediscovering America.* Cambridge, Mass.: Perseus, 1985.

U.S. Census Bureau. "Annual Estimate of Population for Incorporated Places in Oregon." Available www.census.gov/ popest/cities/tables/SUB-EST2003-04-01.pop. Retrieved 1 December 2004.

Vieth, Warren. "US companies pay little or no tax." *Los Angeles Times* 9 April 2004. Available smh.com.au.

Walth, Brent. *Fire at Eden's Gate: Tom McCall and the Oregon Story.* Portland: Oregon Historical Society Press, 1994.

White, Richard. *The Organic Machine: The Remaking of the Columbia River.* New York: Hill and Wang, 1995.

Williams, Walter E. "Education's decline revisited." *Washington Times* 18 Dec 2004. Available washingtontimes. com/commentary/20041217-084901-1674r.htm.

Winterson, Jeanette. *Art and Lies.* New York: Vintage/Random, 1996.

Wortman, Sharon Wood. *The Portland Bridge Book.* Portland: Oregon Historical Society Press, 2001.

Index

affordable housing, 74-77

Beaverton, Ore., 47, 53, 92
Bermingham, Anna, 73
Body Vox, 13
Boring, Ore., 14, 84
Brophy, Michael, 13
Burton, Mike, 101
Bush, George W., 36, 79, 99

Calvino, Italo, 84-90
Chattanooga, Tenn., 81
City Club of Portland, 13
Clackamas County, Ore., 79
Clackamas River, 1, 90, 97
Clark County, Wash., 76-77
Columbia River, 1, 59, 67, 69-70, 84, 96-97
community, 55-59, 77-78, 99, 102, 104-5
    achieved by cooperation, 2-3
    and taxation, 57-58, 99
    as "commons," 59-60
    difficulty of, 55-59, 99
    rewards of, v, 10.
    See also individualism
Country Village, 74-75, 77, 79
Callenbach, Ernest, 72-73
Calvino, Italo, 84-90
Cooper Mountain Vineyards, 5

Dairy Creek, 52
Damascus, Ore., 11, 39, 65, 84, 101
democracy, 36, 44, 45, 55, 60, 77, 96, 97, 102, 104, 105
Detroit, Mich., 57
Dewey, John, 56

English, Dorothy, 100
Epstein, Richard, 98

Florida, Richard, 76

Gandhi, Mohandas K., 38
Gioia, Dana, 10
Goldschmidt, Neil, 103
Gresham, Ore., 6, 84, 96, 101
growth management. See Urban Growth Boundary; sprawl
growth, smart. See smart growth

Happy Valley, 7, 11, 84
Hardin, Garret, 59
Hayes, Stephen, 13
Hillsboro, Ore., 52, 63, 84
Hood River, Ore., 100
housing. See affordable housing; Portland, Ore., housing prices in

individualism, 2, 9-10, 51, 55-60, 77, 79, 97-99, 100, 105
Iraq War, 34-37

Jacobs, Jane, 103
Jackson Bottom Wetlands, 103
Johanson, Brian, 13
Johnson Creek, 16
Johnson, Linda K., 13

Kanne, Jim, 72
Kelbaugh, Douglas, 4, 102-03
Kerry, John, 79, 100
King, Martin Luther, Jr., 38, 56
Kunstler, James Howard, 4

Land Conservation and Development Commission (LCDC), 3
LeGuin, Ursula K., 13
Leopold, Aldo, 58-59
libertarianism. See Libertarian Party; individualism
Libertarian Party, 98
Lippard, Lucy, 4
Los Angeles, 8-9, 12, 13, 76, 82

Map of Disappearing Streams, 104
McCall, Tom, 64, 93, 103
Measure 7, 45, 98, 100-101
Measure 37, 4, 79, 96-102
Metro (government), 2, 3, 39, 75, 100, 101-4
Moses, Robert, 103
Mt. Hood, 29, 30, 90
Mount St. Helens, 28
Muir, John, 26-31, 73, 78
Multnomah County, 100

new urbanism. See smart growth; Urban Growth Boundary; urban planning

1000 Friends of Oregon, 42, 63-64
Oregon City, Ore., 42, 74, 84

Pink Martini, 13
planning, Oregon's land-use, 3, 63, 74,
    78, 91, 92, 93, 95, 97, 105. *See also* urban
    planning
Portland, Ore., 12-13, 14, 27, 29, 30, 32,
    39, 42, 47, 62, 74, 80, 82, 85-87, 91, 92,
    100
    and building codes, 20
    and community, 9, 13, 58, 60, 62
    housing prices in, 7, 75-76, 77
    Port of, 39, 96
    quality of life, 1, 2, 3, 4, 6, 7, 8, 13, 15, 49,
        51, 61, 68, 76-77, 78, 79, 81
    and UGB, 1-3, 6, 11, 12, 14, 17, 22, 40-41,
        49, 65, 68, 69, 83, 91, 96.
    See also Metro; suburbs

Reagan, Ronald, 52-53, 55
Reed College, 65, 91-92
"Reed's Crossing." *See* "St. Mary's"
rivers. *See* Clackamas; Columbia; Sandy;
    Tualatin; Willamette
Riverside, Calif., 76
Rock Creek, 80
Rodriguez, Mark, 56

Sacramento, Calif., 57, 58, 76
"St. Mary's" parcel, 48, 63-66, 101
Sandy River, 1, 39, 67-69, 84, 96, 97
San Diego, Calif., 76
San Jose, Calif., 76
Seattle, Wash., 76
Shepard, Paul, 47-51
Sherwood, Ore., 32-38, 84
smart growth, 3, 63, 64, 101. *See also*
    Urban Growth Boundary, urban
    planning
Spanbauer, Tom, 13
sprawl, 8, 49, 57-58, 82. *See also* suburbs
Springwater Corridor Trail, 39
Stafford, William, 13
Stehekin, Wash., 18
suburbs, 6-8, 54
    Federal policies encouraging, 57-58
Svoboda, Tomas, 13

Thomas, Lewis, 97
Thoreau, Henry David, 32, 37-38, 104
Tran, Minh, 13
Tualatin River, 1, 18, 104

Urban Growth Boundary (UGB) 3, 53, 78,
    87, 101
    and density, 3, 49-51
    and transit, 43-46
    and housing market, 75-77
    as growth management not growth
        limitation, 3, 101
    creates urban identity, 3-4, 8, 13, 40,
        54, 60
    defined, 1, 3-4
    expansion of, 11, 39, 41, 63-66, 84
    mysterious process of, 45, 88-89, 90, 101
    protecting agricultural lands, 5, 40, 53-
        54, 60, 63-66, 78, 80, 91-95.
    See also smart growth; urban planning
urban planning, 43, 44, 45, 76, 77, 79,
    85-86, 104
    critiques of, 41, 42-46, 75-77.
    See also Measure 7, Measure 37
utopia, 4, 71-73, 84-88, 90

Vancouver, B.C., 42, 43
Vancouver, Wash., 76-77
Viet Nam War, 35, 37
vineyards. *See* wine industry

Wallowa Lake, 100
Watts, Alan, 11
Whyte, William, 44
Willamette River, 1, 18, 84, 96, 97
wine industry, 5, 91-95

Yamhill County, 100
Young, Coleman, 57

zoning. *See* urban planning